EXTRAORDINARY
WEALTH

MARK MURPHY

EXTRAORDINARY WEALTH

THE GUIDE TO FINANCIAL FREEDOM
& AN AMAZING LIFE

Printed in the United States of America.

10 9 8 7 6 5 4 3 2 1

ISBN: 978-1-949639-48-3
LCCN: 9781949639483

Book design by Carly Blake.

I dedicate this book to everyone who wants to be a little better version of themselves tomorrow than they were today. We thank the readers for allowing us to be at our best when we are serving others. Finally, my sons Lucas and Bennett Murphy are the source of my inspiration and aspiration.

Table of Contents

CHAPTER 1

It's Not About Assets

People planning for their financial future tend to focus on assets. Their advisors are saying, "Okay, we're going to make sure you have $3 million in your retirement plan." Or they'll set a goal of having $2 million in a brokerage account. But it's not enough to talk about assets. What's most important is ensuring highly reliable streams of income emerge from those assets. That's how real wealth is created and sustained.

Retirement isn't simply about assets. It's far more important to make sure you will have enough income to cover your lifestyle and do the things you want to do. Many people are misled in retirement. I talk to retired people all the time who think they have a lot of money. But when that money is tied up in their home, or it's in a retirement plan and withdrawals are heavily taxed, or interest rates are virtually zero so they can't get any yield, then it's a problem. In fact, it's a death spiral.

Assets—stocks, bonds, CDs, IRAs, 401(k)s, etc.—are just infla-tion-adjusted holding tanks. I certainly believe in Financial Balance®, and most of my clients have some or all of these assets.[1] Financial institutions, however, have tried to convince people that these holding tanks are creating their wealth. It's not true.

We want to fill up those tanks, but that's not where you're going to create wealth. If inflation is 2 percent and you're earning 2 percent, then you're barely keeping up with inflation. Or maybe you're actually losing money—because

1. you're paying taxes on that 2 percent, and

2. your personal rate of inflation is 4 or 5 percent, sometimes even higher, depending on your expenses and spending habits.

No matter what the government says, we all know that inflation is a personal thing. The cost of everything seems to go up. Gas is higher and food is higher; there are things in your grocery basket that weren't there ten years ago. Because of planned obsolescence we're having to buy a new Apple device every year or two. Property taxes and country club bills go up every year. As a result, merely filling up inflation-adjusted holding tanks is never going to create lasting wealth.

Over the last forty years, money managers have loved showing prospective clients that mountain chart that illustrates how if you invested $10,000 with them in 1972, you'd be worth $72 billion today. It's a farce; nobody's made $72 billion that way. While many institutions tout their brokers as the greatest stock pickers in the

---

1   Financial Balance® is a service mark of The Guardian Life Insurance Company of America® (Guardian), New York, NY 10004. © 2019 Guardian 2019-73909 Exp. 2/21. This material has not been endorsed by Guardian, its subsidiaries, agents, or employees. No representation or warranty, either express or implied, is provided in relation to the accuracy, completeness, or reliability of the information contained herein. Guardian, its subsidiaries, agents, and employees do not provide tax, legal, or accounting advice. Consult your tax, legal, or accounting professional regarding your individual situation.

world, an incredibly high percentage of money managers—around 96 percent; some studies say 99 percent—don't beat the index over a five-year period.

Poor investor behavior is the biggest reason why people don't make money in the market the way that mountain chart would have you believe. Investors are buying when they should be selling, and selling when they should be buying. If the stock market dropped today by 15 or 20 percent, 80 percent of investors would be calling their brokers dying to sell. On the flip side, when the market is booming investors are asking, "Why are you wasting my money in bonds at 2 percent? I got 35 percent from the stock market last year."Eight out of ten investors are buying high and selling low, which is poor investor behavior. When push comes to shove, investors chicken out.

This book is about bucking that trend and getting your money to work for you, not the other way around. No matter your position—business owner, executive, or an employee of a corporation—given hard work, enough time, and the right coaching, you can create extraordinary wealth. You *can* do it, but you must have the discipline to do it. We focus on ensuring our clients have the life they want now supported by lasting income and consistent wealth.

WHO THIS BOOK IS FOR

This book is for executives, employees of large corporations, and owners of substantial businesses. My clients are people who have an entrepreneurial spirit and the discipline to create real, lasting wealth. You don't get there by racking up credit card debt; you get there by hiring yourself as your own chief financial officer.

A big part of my strategy is empowering my clients to take control of their financial future. As your own CFO, you are in control. We strategize so your financial goals and your life goals work together. Filling up inflation-adjusted holding tanks is only one part of that.

I wrote this book so you can see the difference in our strategy versus the "wirehouses." You don't want to hire a financial advisor who hasn't created independent wealth for him or herself, yet there are so many CPAs and financial advisors dealing with people who have extraordinary wealth but have never created it themselves.

One of the reasons I am uniquely qualified to be an advisor to small, closely held businesses is because I've done it myself: I've made payroll every two weeks for the last thirty-three years. I've been through all the trials and tribulations. When you've done that yourself, you walk the walk instead of simply selling financial products.

These big financial institutions want your business, but many clients are getting the wrong advice from them and are thus focusing on the wrong things—e.g., whatever product or commodity the firm is pushing, filling up inflation-adjusted holding tanks, expecting to get a high-percentage yield from the market. You can't tell me that advisors at one of the major custodians are superior to advisors at the others. Or that one insurance company's products are better than another's. If they're better this year, then they'll be worse next year because their brokers are selling a commodity as opposed to what cannot be commoditized.

The average person who works in financial services sees seventeen new people a year. They count a husband and wife as two and three partners in a bakery as three. At my firm, Northeast Private Client Group, our phone is ringing every day with people wanting to do business with us because we're not just selling financial products.

A client's total financial picture simply cannot be commoditized. We know this because we've walked the walk ourselves. Our credibility comes from having done exactly what we're teaching our clients to do. It's clearly the differentiating factor. If we don't do it ourselves, we don't teach it.

* * *

I've worked with a lot of doctors and dentists over the last twenty-five years. The biggest compliment they give me is when I'm talking to them and they ask, "Are you a doctor?" They hear that I speak their language and know their business.

In this book, I'm branching out from medical professionals because most of my business does not come from doctors or dentists. Rather, it comes from people who own substantial businesses, corporate executives, and families of significant wealth, as well as entrepreneurs and celebrities. My firm helps people from all walks of life create real, lasting, extraordinary wealth.

My firm helps people from all walks of life create real, lasting, extraordinary wealth.

Another niche of mine is professional athletes. I work with a lot of NFL players. I can't help them be more successful on the field, because I'm not a coach or a trainer. But I can help them plan for their life after football. The time to start thinking about life after football is the day they sign their first contract. A shocking 78 percent of professional athletes are in severe financial distress or bankrupt within two years of retirement.[2] I pound that statistic into my clients. I have a shorthand where I say, "Joe, are you in the 22 percent or the 78 percent? I only work with the 22 percent. Don't go 78 on me, Joe." It's kind of a joke, but it drives

---

2   Serena van Ramele, Haruhito Aoki, Gino Kerkhoffs, and Vincent Gouttebarge, "Mental health in retired professional football players: 12-month incidence, adverse life events and support," *Psychology of Sport and Exercise* 28 (November 2016), doi: 10.1016/j.psychsport.2016.10.009.

home the point. They know what that means.

As soon as they start their career—and this applies to Fortune 500 executives and business owners as well as it does to NFL players—we work on strategies to make them have a better life now, keep that life once they retire, and never run out of money.

BEAT THE MARKET?
MIGHT AS WELL GO TO VEGAS

There are three main reasons why the market isn't as productive as financial institutions would have you believe:

1. fees are too high,

2. they fail to factor in taxes, and

3. they don't take inflation into account.

In the perfect world of the mountain chart, where you're getting 7, 8, or 9 percent yield on your money, that pristine scenario doesn't consider fees, taxes, or inflation. When you factor in those things, you're getting more like 2 percent on your money. The mountain chart is deeply misleading. If you're getting only 2 percent, then you're treading water, or even behind the curve, because you're just keeping up with inflation. Couple that with poor investor behavior and the picture gets even uglier.

If your strategy is to beat the market, you might as well go to Vegas. That's really the strategy many people follow: take everything you've got—all your retirement money, all your cash—go to Vegas, put it on the craps table, and consistently beat the house. And people wonder why they never seem to get ahead.

Say you have $1 million in a conservative portfolio and are counting on withdrawing 4 percent, or $40,000, a year. Some economics reports say retirees can safely draw down 4 percent a year without running out of money; others say it's more like 2.5 percent. For this example, we're using the aggressive number of 4 percent.

Over the last seventy-five years there have been approximately eight retrenchments in the S&P 500, averaging a 38.5 percent loss.[3] We haven't had one in nine years now, but the trend points to one happening every half dozen or so years. When that retrenchment happens, which it does every cycle, your portfolio value drops from $1 million to $600,000. If you're still taking $40,000 a year, now you're pulling out 6.67 percent. After a few years, you no longer have $600,000—you have $400,000. It's a death spiral.

That's what the picture looks like at an aggressive 4 percent. Yet some financial advisors are telling their clients to take out even more—5, 6, or 7 percent. Or, their clients decide themselves to pull out that percentage because they need it to pay for their lifestyle. They have homeowners' association fees, medical bills, and other expenses, so they need more than 4 percent. Then their plans blow up. This death spiral happens to so many people.

It's not much sounder a plan than going to Vegas with your strategy to beat the house. There's nothing illegal or unethical about the beat-the-market strategy, but people are misled into thinking it's a logical plan. It's like saying, "I'm going to hit the slots and come home rich." It could happen, but the odds are almost nil.

THREE LEVELS OF WEALTH

There are three levels of wealth creation. This book teaches you how to progress through levels one and two and ultimately reach the third

---

3   "11 historic bear markets," NBC News, accessed April 17, 2019, http://www. nbcnews.com/id/37740147/ns/business-stocks_and_economy/t/historic-bear-markets/#.XLdMUetKhQK.

level, which is creating multigenerational wealth. But, based on our own experience in the financial planning industry, very few Americans reach even the first level.

Level one

You have enough passive income from your assets to replace your paycheck when you stop working. Reaching this level means you have a stable retirement.

Level two

You have free capital or "playchecks," which are income-producing assets that are not responsible for maintaining your lifestyle. Reaching this level means you have financial freedom.

Level three

You have earned income beyond retirement and continue to earn substantially more than you spend. Reaching this level means you have multigenerational wealth.

The first level is having enough passive income from investments to replace your income from working. If most people in this country can't write a check for $1,000, the idea that those people could get to level three is absurd. Level one is the first goal. It's important to acknowledge that such a small percentage of people can even get there, indicating the kind of planning, discipline, and work ethic required to reach level one.

Instead of getting to level one, some folks try to create financial stability in retirement by working longer than they planned. They extend their careers whether they like what they're doing or not, working past retirement age to maintain their lifestyle because their assets don't produce enough income to replace their paychecks. In a moment, I'll give an example of an accountant who's trying to extend his career for that very reason.

We help our clients develop a plan that provides highly reliable streams of income, and we design those streams of income to replace the client's paycheck from their nine-to-five. But we don't want all their assets huffing and wheezing trying to produce enough income to cover their expenses. That's why we help clients develop a second level of assets. These are "playchecks," a term we borrow from retirement expert, Tom Hegna.

Having playchecks, or free capital, is level two of wealth creation. The money these assets produce plays no role in supporting the client's lifestyle. Playchecks can be spent and enjoyed—or given away. People who reach level two can do whatever they want with the income from these assets because, having reached level one, they've already covered the income they received while working. If you can reach level two, then you have financial freedom.

The third level is having enough money that you can pass it along to the next generation. To create multigenerational wealth, you must have substantially more income than what you're consuming in retirement. There are three ways to get earned income beyond your working years: investing in your business or other operating companies, real estate, or financing deals. All produce income in perpetuity. As you progress through this book, I'll teach you how to get involved in one or more of these strategies.

In an ideal world, all my clients would continue to produce earned income after they retire because that's how you create multigenerational wealth. But not everybody can generate earned income after they retire. That's okay. Set your sights on level one. The idea is to start gathering assets today that will yield highly reliable streams of income to replace your paycheck when you stop working.

Many people would love to reach that first level. Sadly, almost no one does. If my readers just got to level one, I would consider that a huge success.

If you're dedicated and disciplined, this book will teach you how to get to level three. But the reality is, continuing earned income beyond retirement is just not feasible for everyone. Some companies, for example, have a mandatory retirement age. I know a successful accountant whose firm's retirement age is sixty-seven. He's a few years away, and as one of the leaders of the firm he's trying to figure out if he can extend that from sixty-seven to seventy. Although he's done well, he's had significant expenses including raising and paying to educate three children. At sixty-seven, he will not have a large enough nest egg to pay for retirement.

He's not alone, of course. That's why you're seeing a lot of people continue to work beyond retirement age. Some do because they're happy and love what they do, but an awful lot of people continue to work because their lifestyle would fall off a cliff if they didn't have earned income. It's a sad picture: older folks still working every day not because they want to, but because they must. If that accountant hit the lottery, he'd be ready to retire today. He continues to work because his lifestyle would collapse otherwise.

Going to work, putting in your hours, and getting a paycheck is trading your time for dollars. The ways to create lasting wealth, however, do not involve your paid labor. Real wealth is largely created through passive investments. Remember that there are many places to put your money—stocks, bonds, CDs, IRAs, 401(k)s, mutual funds, money market accounts—but these are merely inflation-adjusted holding tanks. The objective isn't just having these tanks filled up; it's getting them to produce highly reliable streams of income that replace your nine-to-five paycheck. The objective is getting to level one.

FOUR PARAMETERS TO CREATING EXTRAORDINARY WEALTH

To reach level one and possibly beyond, you need to follow some basic parameters. It's about discipline. Before you run, you must walk first.

The first parameter involves these three rules:

1. live within your means;

2. save 15 percent or more of your gross income every year (this number is flexible—more on that below); and

3. protect yourself against lawsuits, creditors, disability, permanent loss of income, and death.

Living within your means, saving money, and having proper insurance coverage are nonnegotiable if you want to get to level one, let alone two or three. I wrestle with people every day who are making $300,000 or $500,000, even $1 million or $2 million a year, and can't put away 15 percent of their pretax income. One family, for example, had $600,000 in annual income. They moved to a nicer house, spent a ton on renovations, and now they can't pay their bills. Yet I see on Facebook that they're on vacation. To be a good financial advisor, one of my first jobs is to get my clients to live within their means. None of the rest is possible if you're not going to live within your means.

The second parameter is understanding that it's all about liquidity. Many people have money tied up in their business, real estate, and retirement plans, but they can't write a check for any meaningful amount of money. Liquidity allows you to make intelligent, long-term decisions.

The third parameter is hiring yourself as your own CFO. Like the family above, many people spend more time planning vacations than they do planning their finances. To create real wealth, *you* must lead the process. I hope you're reading this book because you're ready to commit to being your own CFO. Rather than outsourcing wealth management to a CPA or financial planner, you empower yourself.

The fourth parameter is not having bad debt. Good debt—low-cost, tax-deductible, fixed debt—is acceptable. Other types of debt are not.

I sit down with some people who say, "Mark, I've got no money to save. I just can't save any money." Sure enough, they have $30,000 of credit card bills at 20 percent interest. Just the interest on that is $6,000 a year. That's $500 a month they could save if they weren't paying Visa.

Look, to do what this book is about you've got to quit paying the credit card companies so much money. You've got to take care of that debt and start living within your means.

You must also protect yourself and your family with proper insurance coverage. Here's an example of how important it is to have protection for yourself and your family. I'm from Summit, New Jersey, a town that lost eleven people on 9/11. Within two years, all those families had moved away. Summit was where they wanted to raise their kids, but they could no longer afford it. They didn't have enough life insurance or assets saved, so they had to move somewhere with lower property values and lower-quality schools. The tragic losses those families suffered were multiplied, because they didn't have the proper protection.

Starting with these four parameters, extraordinary wealth is in reach. You take small steps, one by one, to build the future you want.

FINANCES ARE LIKE DIETING: SMALLS CHANGES CREATE BIG RESULTS

Following those four parameters demands a lifestyle change for many people. I'm not saying you must start saving huge amounts of money right away. Not at all. I don't know what your mortgage is, what your rent is, or what it costs to raise your kids. I don't know what your bills are. So, I'm not going to say to you, "You've got to save 15 percent or more, and I'd like it to be more like 20 percent, 25 percent, or 30 percent." You'll look at me like I'm crazy because maybe you can't save anything right now.

That's okay. We won't start there. We start by making a smaller change. Can we save 7 percent? Can we save 5 percent? Can we save 3 percent? Small moves over the long term create big results.

I compare this to dieting. My whole adult life I've struggled with my weight. I've learned that crash diets never work because they're not sustainable. The financial equivalent of a crash diet is someone who's saying, "Okay, we're going to save lots of money here and here and here." But a year later, they're doing nothing because putting all that money into savings would choke them to death. They couldn't live on it.

Instead of a crash diet, what works for people is a lifestyle change. The only people who are successful in the dieting world are people who change how they live. They change how they eat and how they move their body. They change their mentality and start thinking like a healthy person.

It's the same strategy with money. You've got to start thinking like a rich person. It's a lifestyle change that starts with investing in yourself.

CHAPTER 2

Invest In ...Yourself

When I'm giving talks around the country, I have a slide titled "If I'm a great financial coach, I will coach our clients to ..." One of the bullet points on this slide is "pay yourself first."

Investing in yourself is the first thing any entrepreneur should do. If you have a business and you're going to save one dollar, the best investment entrepreneurs can make is in themselves. The big brokerage houses are trying to convince you that giving that dollar to them—so a money manager can invest it in one of the vehicles they provide—is the smartest choice.

I strongly disagree. The best thing to do is invest that dollar in yourself. Grow your business. Grow your ROI. Take that dollar and continue to grow.

We coach our clients to follow the same principle of investing in themselves, whether they're business owners or employees. If I'm a great financial coach, I get my clients to think many moves ahead. I'm a master bridge player and competitive chess player, so I've been trained to think moves ahead. In bridge, you play all thirteen tricks out in your mind before you lay down the first one. In chess, you think eight moves ahead.

It's the same idea in the investment world. Whether you're a student, an associate in a law firm, or an employee at a Fortune 500 company, try to think thirteen tricks or eight moves ahead. Try to figure out where you want to be down the road. Then, let's navigate that road so you can get there.

In my thirty-three years in this business, I can't think of a single entrepreneur who didn't say that the best investment he or she ever made was investing in themselves. As an entrepreneur myself, I say ditto to that.

INVEST IN YOUR EDUCATION

One of the best ways to invest in yourself is to make sure you have the proper education. Some clients tell me that they want to be an executive vice president or the president of one of the major divisions in their company. Often one of the requirements, whether it's implicit or explicit, is having an MBA.

Do you have the right education to get where you want to be? The right leadership skills, training, contacts? Or is this the kind of job you can't attain in this company? In certain industries, you need to hopscotch among employers to get that promotion you're looking for.

It's so important for people to really think through where they want to be in the future. With my NFL clients, I talk to them about how everybody's excited about pro sports and pro athletes—and why they should capitalize on that and start creating opportunities for themselves now, while they're in their prime and have the cachet of fame. The day they sign their first contract is the time for them to start thinking about life after football.

For example, some want to be in the real estate business after their NFL career. So, in the offseason, we help them get internships with major real estate companies. Of course, the companies love having an NFL player as an intern.

I tell these clients, "You're probably going to have to go to a few dinners with some of the big clients or partners, but you're going to get a great education in these two months. If we do this every year in the offseason, by the time you're in the second half of your football career and getting ready to step away, you won't be starting at a standstill. You're going to be running into this new career. You're going to be *at least* as successful as you were on the field."

I can't help athletes get better at playing football. That's not what I do. What I can do is help them do all the things to prepare for life after football. In fact, these steps—hard work, training, perseverance—are similar to what's helped them succeed as a professional athlete. We have them work on that same skill set. That way, they're preparing for their second career in the same way they've spent years preparing for football.

BOARD POSITIONS AND OTHER WAYS OF MOVING UP

As a financial advisor, do I think it's important that we try to get our clients 10 percent on their money instead of 9 percent? Of course. I think it's very important that they're in the proper investments and getting the proper return.

But it's far more important that we help them achieve that next position in their field. We want our clients to have the best, most appropriate investments in their portfolio, but it's far more important that they invest in themselves—that they think thirteen tricks or eight moves ahead and plan for where they next want to be in their career.

People aren't doing that. Our goal is to get people to think geometrically, rather than arithmetically, about their careers. That gives them the chance to get what they want. That's how they're going to get ahead.

As employees ascend to more senior roles in big companies, those businesses often like their leaders to have experience outside their company. So, we've gotten involved with helping those clients find board positions at other companies and in other industries. Most companies want their senior officers to sit on at least one outside board to broaden their experience and knowledge and fill out their résumés. Then, when they're ready to become the president of that division, managing partner, or the CEO of that company, they're fully prepared and informed. We help them do that.

We also do that for senior people who are on the way out. They're nearing retirement, possibly trimmed their hours, and they say, "I'm no longer working three thousand hours a year, but I'm smart and I can still contribute to companies." We help them set up a board seat that will pay a few hundred thousand dollars a year, provide some fun, and allow them to use all the valuable wisdom they've built up over their careers.

Sometimes investing in yourself professionally means something besides serving on an outside board. If the client is a partner in a law firm, we might figure out how we can get them named to the executive committee, chairman of their department, or maybe managing partner of the whole firm.

LIFESTYLE INVESTMENTS

Sometimes investing in yourself is a lifestyle issue. We have clients who, when they start thinking many moves ahead, are thinking about their kids' education. For example, we help them figure out how to get their kids into the right private high school or college.

Another area that's often overlooked by money managers is what's going on in a client's marriage. I've been saying for the last thirty years, "One of the keys to wealth is to meet your second spouse first." What do I mean by this? Well, I often have conversations with success-ful, busy people who are in the throes of marriage, raising children, and growing their career. I remind them that what's happening in their marriage is integral to their financial future.

I'll say, "Look, since we got together last time, I've seen great strides in your career and great strides with you financially. I think you've invested well. But, as somebody who is close to you, it seems to me that you're not investing in your marriage or your family in the way you told me you'd like to be. Maybe it's time to take your spouse away for a long weekend or surprise them in some way. I realize it's tough when you've been in a long-term relationship, but remember the only behavior we can control is our own. I know you're committed to this. You focused on your career and look at the results you got. You paid attention to your investments and look at the results you got. But you haven't made the same commitment to or investment in your relationship.

"It's time to do that because that's just as important to your success in life—maybe even more important. It's also just as important

19

to your financial success. As a couple, you want to make sure that you and your spouse are always on the same page in every way."

Helping clients invest in themselves in this way—so they're creating life balance along with Financial Balance®—means we're no longer just their money manager. We're much more than that.

To be clear, money management is something we do very well. But it's only one of twenty-three things we do. Insurance advisory is another one of twenty-three things we do, and we do that damn well too. Our expertise in that area is important because so few people do that well, but that's still not the secret sauce.

The secret sauce is to think about the life you want. That's what makes this career so rewarding for my team and me: listening.

As our physician and dentist clients say, diagnosis without examination is malpractice. It's the same in our business. We really listen to people and help them get what they want—not what we think they want, but what they want for their lives. As a great financial coach, I take the time to understand my clients so that we can develop not just a financial plan or a business plan, but a life plan. Then, all aspects of their lives are working together.

For example, some of my lawyer clients have no aspiration to become managing partner of their law firm. They don't want the pressure of being in that position. They want to get home at 5:00 p.m. or 6:00 p.m. every day, see their spouse, and be on the Little League field with their kids. I have dentist clients who are happy with a dental practice that bills $1 million or $1.5 million a year; they don't want a $5 million or $10 million practice.

Of course, more clients do want to achieve those things than don't because most successful people are alphas. They are used to competing at the highest level, and they want to continue to do that in every area of their life. But many don't.

DEFINE YOUR "WHY"

Most people, most of the time, are in a scarcity mind-set. That's where people are naturally. When you're in a scarcity mind-set, you can only focus on what is and what's in front of you.

Instead, I coach my clients to have an abundance mind-set. I say, "For the next hour or hour and a half that I'm with you, let's get you in an abundance mind-set so we can focus on more than just 'what is.' I know we have to deal with 'what is'; I'm not delusional. But the idea is let's focus on *what could be*. Let's think about the life you want, the business you want, the career you want. And, of course, your family. What if everything was working for you? What would have to happen?"

Or I'll phrase it this way: "If we were to get together three or four or five years from today, what would have had to happen both personally and professionally for you to be wildly satisfied with the results?"

Once we change the narrative to *what could be* instead of *what is*, it's a revelatory moment for many clients. Some tell me, "I didn't think this was possible. I was just going on and on because I didn't realize what could be." It gets them to start thinking about what they're fighting for in their life and what they're really, truly passionate about.

WHAT KIND OF STONECUTTER ARE YOU?

To invest in yourself you must think ahead, know where you want to be, and know why you want to be there. There must be a powerful "why" for you to keep putting in the hard work and have the discipline to create extraordinary wealth.

Ren, a philosopher in the fifteenth century, described three types of stonecutters: the ones who cut stone to feed their families, the ones who cut stone because they were talented and artistic, and the ones who cut stone because they believed they were building a temple for God.

Some people must cut stone to feed their families. That's just reality. But if it's possible for you to cut stone for another reason, it's better if you can find your passion and do it because you believe you're building a temple for God. For example, I have a very successful business and a son who's in college. I don't want him to join my business because he thinks he's going to make a lot of money. I'm only open to him joining the business if he's waking up every day with joy in his heart because he's able to help people change their lives for the better.

Most people spend more time on work than on any other aspect of their life. Sadly, many people are unhappy with what they're doing. They're putting in their time, but they can't wait for the weekend or day off. They're spending eight, ten, or twelve hours a day at work. For some clients, by the time they get done with their commute, it's fourteen or sixteen hours. With the technology we have now, I see people who are never away from work.

Money is only a byproduct or yardstick of success. I don't do it for the money. If you're always chasing money, there's never enough. But if you're chasing a passion, if you're building a temple for God, if you're waking up every day with joy in your heart, you'll never worry about the money.

When I sit down with people who say, "My business is okay," or, "My life is okay," it's because they don't have the "why." They haven't figured out *why* they're doing what they're doing. They do it because they graduated from college and took a job. Now they're on autopilot.

To have the life you want now and have the discipline to keep it that way forever and never run out of money, you must figure out the "why." We help people do that. One of the ironies of my role is meeting people who think they're at the end of their career. Yet once we start defining the "why" and getting them excited about what they do, they don't want to retire. This is particularly true in dentistry. I'll meet with dentists and they'll say, "I'm retiring at the end of next year and moving on." But then, suddenly, we get them excited about the business again, not only because it's growing and they're making more money but because they're learning new things and serving others. I often say to these people, "As long as your clients or patients are people, you're in the people business."

They get reengaged in their relationships. Then they tell me, "No, no, no. I don't want to retire." Or they get upset because before they met me they made an agreement to sell their practice to their junior partner and now they don't want to go. At the time, they were ready. Now, they have a passion again and a reason to be there. They were running into retirement and now they're digging in their heels because they have a "why."

Compare that to just putting in your time and checking the box. If you're just checking the box, you can't get away from that fast enough. If you have a "why," then you're building a temple for God.

DO WHAT YOU LOVE

Twenty years ago, my business coach Dan Sullivan taught me an exercise I share with clients and do myself every six months: get a piece of paper, draw a line down the middle, and make a line across the top to form a "T." On the left side, I write all the things I'd be doing in retirement that I'm not doing right now. On the right side, I write all the things I don't like about my business.

Then I try to add stuff to the left side and get rid of stuff on the right side. For example, I recently bought an oceanfront place in Palm Beach. Fifteen years ago, I stopped driving a car during the week and hired a driver. I haven't written a check in twenty-five years. I don't open mail, and I handle almost no paperwork. I started playing bridge again. Although I don't have time to go to a bridge club, I've been playing bridge online after many years of not doing it.

I try to do only things I love to do and delegate everything else. I've identified my unique ability, so I focus on that and delegate the rest. All I do is shake hands and kiss babies. I build relationships, close deals, and work on the intellectual property of my firm. I don't do anything else.

CHAPTER 3

Invest In ...
Your Business

If you wait and wait to have the life you want, sometimes you never get there. My grandfather is an example. Chairman of the board of Christian Dior, my grandfather worked hard for a long time, made a lot of money, and saved and saved. He finally retired, hoping to have this glorious post-career life. Sadly, he died within three months. He never got to have the life he wanted because he was waiting to retire to have it.

Financial Balance® and life balance need to go together. I ended last chapter talking about the T chart. On the left side, you list all the things you want to be doing in retirement that you're not doing right now. On the right side, you list all the things you don't like about your business. My argument to an entrepreneur is this: let's say you're forty years old and want to retire at sixty-five. If you can start adding things to the left side and getting rid of things on the right, who would want to retire from that?

In a way, you can retire at forty. Why wait until you're sixty-five? Don't wait twenty-five years to have the life you want.

BEGIN WITH THE END IN MIND

Not every reader of this book has their own business. But every reader can invest in their career. For readers who aren't business owners—who don't control their time, who work for someone else or within an organization, but who have an entrepreneurial mind-set—investing in your business starts with deciding where you want to go.

Just like any good business has a strategic plan, any employees looking to progress in their career must have their own strategic plan laying out how they're going to get where they want to go.

Let's say you're a lawyer working at a big firm. The long-term strategy could be ascending from junior partner to senior partner, to senior partner on the executive committee, to managing partner. What are the things we need to do to help you attract more clients and build your book of business? How do we help you put together a marketing plan so you're out there speaking and getting recognized? How do we help you obtain the business development skills needed to move your career forward?

Some firms value teamwork, so being involved in committees is important. Others want you to be known for your expertise in a specific area of law, first within your firm, then outside of it. You can build your reputation by writing articles, doing speaking gigs, and getting the recognition your firm values.

This path is not everyone's cup of tea, of course. Your goal is your goal. It's our job to help you figure out what's possible and what you'd like to do with your life. We identify that goal, then reverse engineer a plan to acquire the skill set needed.

DEVELOPING THE SKILLS

For many employees who want to build their career, how you present yourself to prospective clients is often a critical growth area. Maybe you're not speaking to big groups, but any employee with the goal of elevating their career wants to be able to get in front of other professionals who can refer business. They want to present themselves in a way that allows the audience to say, "You seem smart and trustworthy. You seem like somebody I'd like to work with."

Early in my career, I hired Gail Goodman, an expert in telephone skills training. She coached every one of our people on how to answer the phone. Even if it was ringing off the hook every day, I wanted the phone to always be answered like that was the most important call we'd received all week.

More recently, we've used a group called Heroic Public Speaking. That relationship has not only been good for my employees who do a lot of public speaking; it's been good for everyone. Because all of us talk to clients every day.

As an employee, where do you need to grow to get where you want to be? Maybe you're smart, technically proficient, and a hard worker, but you need better people skills. Maybe it's leadership skills. Are there courses you can take? Are you mentoring or do you have a mentor? Are you in a study group? I've been involved with the same study group for twenty-five years, which has been invaluable to my career. This group created a foundation for the financial advisor I've become. It also created great friendships.

Whether a study group or telephone skills training, it's never the same thing for everyone. Remember our belief that diagnosis without examination is malpractice. Some lawyers don't want to be a managing partner. They have a great life and are happy not to deal with the internal politics of management. Others think their career is a failure if they don't become managing partner. Your specific goals will drive the process of building the skills to get there.

IF YOU HAVE $1 TO INVEST ...

As a business owner, if you have $1 to invest, instead of paying down a loan or putting it into an investment vehicle, let's take that dollar and put it into your business. Investing in your business could generate an exponential rate of return—not only increasing the value of your business but increasing your cash flow for many years to come.

Paying down your debts and putting your money into inflation-adjusted holding tanks are important things we recommend our clients do. We certainly believe in 401(k)s and insurance and paying down debt. But if you have only $1 to invest and you own a business—instead of getting a 2.25 percent return on a loan, or even getting 5, 6, or 7 percent from the market—the best investments entrepreneurs make is when they invest in themselves.

What are some examples of those investments? *Hiring an additional staff person* to free up the entrepreneur's time to focus on their unique ability. I've tried to figure out what my time is worth per hour. While it's more of an art than a science, it's still very instructive. I'm certainly willing to hire somebody I can pay $20 or $30 an hour if my time is worth $1,000 an hour.

Let's say an entrepreneur's time is worth $1,000 an hour. If they have unlimited ability to $1,000-an-hour work, then they want to pay as many people as they can to do $20- or $30-an-hour tasks. Some business owners think they're *saving* money by paying bills themselves, doing clerical work, and making photocopies. They're really costing their company money. Those business owners, if they're entrepreneurs, should hire somebody to do those tasks so they can focus on growing their business.

Sometimes investing in your business means *technology* that will help you grow. Sometimes it means *further training or education* for yourself and your team. Personally, I've spent a lot of time and money getting more education and trying to be the best in my business. I've continued having a thirst for knowledge and learning.

This mind-set has motivated me to seek out coaches throughout my career. I've always thought that's how the best get better. I've had probably a dozen coaches over the years—everyone from a therapist to a business coach and a telephone coach. They've all added value to my business. I never thought that, because I was doing well, that was the time to stop. As the saying goes, "When you're green, you're growing. When you're ripe, you're rotten."

A lot of people seem to think they've arrived. They're barely to first base, yet they think they've hit a home run. Our job is to show them that so much more is possible. We show them that there are so many other things we can work on.

* * *

The amount of education and training you have determines how far you can take your business or career. Dentists, for example, are only able to diagnose within their ability to treat. If they can't do a complicated procedure, then they can't diagnose it. That's universal in any business. Financial advisors who don't understand advanced money-making techniques can't do them and therefore can't recommend them to clients.

Every business has this. If you can become the best and most knowledgeable about what you do, then you can offer a more lucrative menu of services. So, sometimes you spend money on education. Sometimes you spend money on *coaching* to identify your unique ability. Sometimes you spend money on *networking and marketing*. When you're growing a business and times get tough, the one thing people need is clients. Are you putting enough money into marketing to make sure enough people are coming through the door to buy your products or services?

Often, people think by not spending money they're automatically saving money and can therefore be more profitable. They think they're saving money by not doing any marketing. In fact, they're costing their company a fortune. They should be thinking about how they can put together a marketing plan that will double their clients and the size of the business in three years.

Instead, they decide to take that $20,000 and pay down their mortgage at 4.5 percent because they want to pay it off in twenty-nine years instead of thirty. That's not a wealth strategy. Now, am I against paying down your debt? Of course not. I'm for Financial Balance®. I'm for abundance. But if you have only $1 to invest, your business is the first place you want to look. The second, third, and fourth places you want to look are investment accounts, paying down your debts, and all those other things.

The people who, when they have $1 to invest, put that money toward paying down their debts or into broker accounts are doing okay. They're not setting the world on fire; they're just making a living. The people who use it to invest in themselves are the ones who create wealth. The people who make wise investments in themselves see their businesses grow not arithmetically but geometrically.

QUEENS OF BE—*BE, DO, HAVE*

One of the great successes in my career was mentoring four senior managers at an accounting firm. I worked with these women for about five years. Today, all four are partners in major international accounting firms.

At our first mentoring meeting a dozen years ago, I said to them, "I can't do anything about the board of your company—whether they're ever going to make you a partner or not." I had no power to do that. Nor did they. But what I could do is get them thinking about what being a partner would look like. I said, "Let's pretend that I can make you partners in the firm. I want you to *be* a partner today and do the work that a partner does. If you do that, eventually you'll have the title."

This changed their mind-set. Every one of them knew that they *could* do the work of a partner. Thinking that they had to be made partner first was a trap—it never works in that direction. It's always be, then do, then have: *Be* a partner, *do* that work, then *have* the title. I started calling them the "Queens of Be."

It's common thinking to want the title first, then do the work second. If you're truly investing in your career and building out your book of business,

If you're truly investing in your career and building out your book of business, you will *be*, then *do*, then *have*.

you will *be*, then *do*, then *have*. Twelve years later, I still call them Queens of Be, and all four are wildly successful senior partners.

The coaching involved was different for each woman. While all four knew that they could do the work of a partner, each needed to work on different areas to round out their skills. One worked on speaking so she could get up in front of a room and give a talk to a group of potential clients. Another worked on time management—she was raising three young children, so we helped her focus on what she needed to do to be most effective with her time. Another worked on networking and marketing to get in front of more prospective clients.

Everyone is different. Investing in building out one's book of business means something different for every employee out there. Part of the process is understanding each person's unique ability and helping them create a vision of where they want to be. Everyone comes in with things they do well, but also areas that need work. We identify their unique ability, their resources, where they want to go, and then develop the areas that will get them there. Diagnosis without examination is malpractice.

Once the Queens of Be were performing the work of partners, they started coming up with courses and marketing events that the firm's management team was willing to support. The board and executive committee were willing to spend money to promote these women and their ideas.

A PERSONAL LIFE AND A BUSINESS LIFE

You have a personal life and you have a business life. I encourage our clients and employees to have balance in their lives. Of course, balance means something different to everyone.

Last chapter, we talked about lifestyle choices that are an important part of investing in yourself. Likewise, investing in your business or career may also mean a lifestyle investment. They're not always business things. Sometimes the investment that makes the most sense is a personal investment: it's funding your kids' education or getting that swimming pool or beach house. It's helping your grandchildren or other loved ones. It's totally individual.

I have some clients who really want to retire, so we focus on getting to retirement. I have other clients who don't want to retire at all. They're like sharks: they may slow down and spend three days in the office instead of six. They may travel more. But if we make them stop swimming, they'd die.

If you're a shark, it's important to know what's going to make you happy in retirement. I go to South Florida every winter and talk to titans of industry who are now retired. I'll ask how they're doing.

"Well, I used to have eight thousand people report to me and now I go to the dry cleaner's and make dinner reservations."

Whereas another very successful retiree couldn't be happier: "I play golf three days a week and bridge two days a week. We go out to dinner with a group of friends. We're always doing fun stuff. I'm doing everything I never did when I was working. You helped me retire five years earlier than I was planning, so thank you."

Two guys with different objectives. While having balance in life never means the same thing for any two people, we all need to have that balance. At the end of the day, it's never just about money or business. It's about having a great life.

COST EFFICIENCIES

You should have an unlimited appetite for investment and no appetite for expenses. If something is an expense in our business, it's always on the chopping block. If something is an investment in our business, we have an unlimited appetite for it.

My goal is to achieve a return of four to five times on my money, so if I invest $100,000 I'm expecting to get $400,000 or $500,000 back. It's about making the best investments, because every business has finite amounts of money and finite amounts of time and stress they can put on their team.

With finite money and time, we cannot major in minor things. We put our efforts and resources into what we consider the best opportunities. If you do too many things, your team gets diffused and you don't become proficient in anything.

Of course, sound business practice is also part of the equation. I want business owners to make sure they're not overpaying for office supplies, rent, salaries, or anything else. But you never save your way to wealth or profitability.

If I can get a client to grow their business substantially, and it's a business that's desirable, as many of them are, that's a winning formula. That's a way to create wealth. The value of a business, until you sell it, is a number on a piece of paper. You can't touch it until you sell it. But you can significantly grow your income by investing in and growing your business.

Investing in your business is the best investment any entrepreneur can make.

A client with a $5 million business, for example, may be taking out $500,000 in compensation. It's not unusual to see that client grow their business to $10 million in revenue. Now, because of economies and efficiencies of scale, by doubling their business the owner's income doesn't go from $500,000 to $1 million—it goes to $3 million. What investment, via what stock market, can achieve that rate of return? Investing in your business is the best investment any entrepreneur can make.

GO WHERE THE PUCK'S GOING

Entrepreneurs understand that it's not just about thriving but also surviving. Companies like Amazon and Uber have upended entire industries. Nevertheless, entrepreneurs are open to doing what it takes to stay one step ahead. Wayne Gretzky used to say he paid less attention to the puck than where the puck was heading.

Unless you stay that one step ahead of where your industry is going, you're likely to be a casualty or at least continue to struggle. I find many people running businesses using the same strategies and ideas they were using ten, fifteen, or twenty years ago. They're now experiencing a profitability problem. I sit down with them and they'll say, "In the 1990s I was making a very high number. Since then, the business has not really grown. But expenses have crept up. Things have gotten tighter and tougher because there are new competitors and new ideas coming into the marketplace."

Well, that was the state of affairs back in the 1990s. It's 2019 now. And we know that those competitors and their ideas have made a relic out of the method of doing business that was lucrative in the 90s. So, let's look at where the puck is headed.

* * *

Too many people leave their fate to happenstance rather than putting together a plan. From all the work that we've done helping so many people from different walks of life plan for their financial future, the people who have truly thought about it—who have a defined plan to get the job or accomplish their goal—are much more successful at achieving those goals than the people who have an attitude of, "I'm just gonna show up, keep working, and see what happens."

Having a defined plan for investing in one's career is so much more powerful. It's not going to happen by happenstance. It's going to happen through a deliberate plan.

CHAPTER 4

Invest In ... Your People

I take great pride in the people who have worked for me over the years at Northeast Private Client Group. Their employment with this company has allowed them to pay their mortgages, send their kids to college, and live the life they want.

People have a special place in my business. It's all about the relationships. I think about my employees the same way I think about clients: we're not only in the financial services business, we're also in the people business. And just as we work to provide clients with direction, creativity, and companionship along their path to financial freedom, we also work to provide those same pillars of support to our employees.

YOU'RE ONLY AS GOOD AS YOUR TEAM

There's only one of you and only so many working hours in the day. For you to be an entrepreneur, grow a business, and have a life, you must have great people around you. That's as important as anything else in an entrepreneur's world.

The objective is to build an unstoppable team that gets along and works together. Part of being a great leader is showing your team what a great job looks like. If you succeed at that, then over time it'll begin to look like you're working for them, not the other way around.

I get a lot of joy from what we've been able to create—supporting families, educating kids, and doing purposeful work. At the same time, it's still a business. I must make sure to get a return on my money.

From the standpoint of investing in my business, I want to hire the very best people out there. While any business owner invests in people the same way they invest in, say, new software (i.e., by spending money), I would never conflate a human being with technology. Yet when I hire someone, I am looking for the same return as with any other investment in my business: four or five times on my money. If I pay you $100,000, down the line I want to recoup $400,000 or $500,000.

In addition to showing my people what a great job looks like, I also need to create an environment where people can identify their unique ability and focus on that at least 80 percent of the time. If you can get employees to capitalize on their unique ability, then you have something powerful. Everybody is on the same page, using the same transformational language that gets a predictable result every time.

We use this principle in our approach to client relationships, but it's our policy internally as well. Early in my career, however, instead of providing a "wow" experience to both clients and employees, I was more one-dimensional—always bending over backward for clients and treating them like gold. But our business really took off when I gave that same level of care and compassion to our employees. Not that I wasn't good to them before; I just wasn't creating the same sense of caring and excitement. That was an epiphany for me that changed our business radically.

CREATING A "WOW" EXPERIENCE FOR YOUR PEOPLE

An entrepreneur knows every wart and pimple on his or her business. The shocking thing is that every single employee knows them as well. If your company isn't performing, then you're at risk of losing your best people. If you have several years in a row when you're not growing your business, your best people are either going to be looking for opportunities elsewhere or other employers are going to poach them. Staying with you would stifle their ability to grow. A company not doing well financially doesn't have the resources to pay the best people. They may *want* to pay them; they just don't have the resources to do it because their business is not performing at that level.

Being more transparent with my team created that "wow" experience for them. In turn, our business grew. Transparency meant being much clearer about where the business was going and how their individual roles contributed to the bigger picture. We took the time to show them all the issues with our clients. Everyone learned how their role was important to the process; they saw that they weren't just punching a clock. When people could start to see the bigger picture—not just what they were doing but *why* they were doing it—that made all the difference in how our employees thought about their roles. They brought a new level of motivation to their work.

Our business grew significantly as a result. My team now understood the links in the chain. When somebody did a great job servicing a client and preparing for a meeting to go over that client's portfolio, and we had that "wow" meeting, they could see how important they were to that experience. The opposite was also illustrative. If someone did not do a great job servicing a client or preparing for that meeting, and it did not go as well as it could have, then they could see that they were directly responsible for how that business turned out.

With greater transparency, our team understood how every role had an impact. For example, because things in the securities and insurance worlds can drag on (underwriting, paperwork, transfers—all kinds of issues that cause delays), the underwriting department saw that if we could cut our time onboarding a client, say from two or three months to four or five weeks, then the client stayed engaged. During the shorter onboarding the client remained excited, as opposed to the months-long version where time stretched out and it became necessary to reengage the client in the process.

We also included the staff in what was going on behind the scenes with clients. This made it much more purposeful work. They could see that they weren't just investing money or buying insurance; they were helping our clients lead better lives. They became emotionally attached to the success of the clients, whether they were helping them buy that new home or grow a business. They now had real relationships with our clients. They were changing clients' lives for the better and could genuinely believe that they were part of that. It became more of a mission than a job.

"A" PLAYERS COMPARED TO "B" AND "C" PLAYERS

As entrepreneurs, we know that the best investments we make is when we invest in ourselves. Expenses are always on the chopping block, while we have an unlimited appetite for investments. Ultimately, we invest in employees with a master plan of growing the business and creating a better experience for clients.

Excellent human capital is hard to come by, which is why it's such a valuable area of investment. It's so challenging to get people who not only have a high IQ, but also a high EQ—not only emotional intelligence but also people smarts and street smarts. Common sense, ironically, is not too common in our world. You need people with intelligence, people skills, and a high degree of common sense.

When you find people who have those attributes, you can figure out how to get that four or five times return with them. Some of the best people we've hired over the years were not hired to fill a specific job; we just ran across somebody who had those qualities and knew they would bring value to our company. Those are such rare qualities that we knew we could train those people to do a great job. Those people are "A" players.

If people don't get it right away, you continue to work with them. If they continue not to get it, they often self-select themselves out or you ask them to leave. How long are you willing to tolerate people who aren't getting the job done? You can't tolerate poor performance over any reasonable period. You owe it not just to yourself and your business but also to those other employees out there working hard for you every day. You owe it to the people who *do* get it not to let people who *don't* get it stay around over the long term. If you allow people to stay who aren't performing and don't seem able to improve, all you do is download their work onto your good people. That makes life a lot harder for the people who are really doing the job. That's not fair.

When you have people who aren't doing what you need them to do, you must counsel them out of the business. Because if they're not getting it, they're not going to be successful long-term. They're not going to get the raises and bonuses that other people get. But more importantly, you want to make sure that you're not unduly burdening your best employees. We're all guilty of this. We need something done for an important client, so who are we going to give it to? Our best employee or worst employee? Somebody we have confidence in, who will do whatever it takes to get that thing done, or somebody who will get it done when they're ready?

Say one of your employees is soaking up every bit of knowledge and trying to figure out how they can add more and more value to your business. Another is worrying about whether you're shutting down at two o'clock or three o'clock the day before Thanksgiving. Look, I think it's great to have plans for the holiday. That's not the issue. But if the main discussion we're having is what time the office is closing for Thanksgiving, then we're probably not having conversations about how they can improve and make the client experience that much better. It's very telling. Those people are going to be "B" and "C" players, or maybe not there at all.

LET THE BOSS KNOW

One of the smartest things an employee can do is let their boss know that they're ready to play full out. As a CEO myself, sometimes that's the only way I will know. People who own companies are very busy. Often, they don't know what they themselves are doing all day, let alone every employee.

You don't want to be a suck up or known as a self-promoter, but it's important that, in an elegant way, you find out how to really let your boss know what you're doing and how you're bringing value to the business. Let them know you're playing full out and want to be great. Get a little buy-in from the company's owner. When I hear from our team, I often am not aware of all the great things they have been doing. As a boss, not only do I get to understand what they're doing, I also get to weigh in on what they could be doing even better.

I find that people often have the best intentions and are doing what they think is best for the company, but they're slightly askew. I've had people in my company who were giving everything they had, they were just focusing on the wrong things. Having that direct conversation with the boss takes all the mystery out of it—you can figure out what they're getting right and what they're getting wrong. Then, they can be more efficient so they're not confusing motion for productivity. They can give the same full-out energy they've always given. Only now, they're doing it in the most productive way.

TRAINING: HOW THE BEST GET BETTER

We are constantly finding seminars and webinars for our people to get involved in. In the last chapter I mentioned the company Heroic Public Speaking, which we initially used solely for our sales staff. We've since gotten our entire team involved. We want to have people capable of presenting themselves and our company in the best way possible.

Investing in your people means encouraging them to keep growing.

Investing in your people means encouraging them to keep growing. I encourage my team to not only *be* the best they can today, but also to *continue* training, which is something we're always willing to invest in. We've invested in coaches, for example—anything we can do so the best can get better. Even if you're great at your job, either you're green and growing or ripe and rotten. There's no in-between.

The idea is to never be satisfied. There's always another level. We've always believed that for everybody—ourselves, our clients, our individual employees—life is just a series of S-curves. If, for one of our people, that S-curve is starting to turn down, we help them figure out how to create another path.

I say to my staff, "I want other people to want to hire you. I want to have to compete for your services because you're adding so much value to our company that I've got to pay you more and more and more. Figure out ways I've got to pay you more to keep you happy and keep you locked into our company."

The person I don't want to hire is the person who can't get a job anywhere else because nobody else sees the value in what they do. For employees, it's about capability. I want to make my employees even more marketable than they are now. I want them to have even more capability than they have now. Employees want to get paid more every year, so let's figure out how to develop more capability for them.

If you continue to do purposeful work, grow your business, and pay employees properly, then ideally they will start regarding your business as just as much theirs as it is yours. And people will want to stay there because you have that "wow" experience every day; you create that experience for clients, and you contribute to changing people's lives for the better.

The people who just do the same old thing in this economy will get commoditized. Their expenses will rise, their revenue will shrink, and eventually they won't be a very attractive company. My company has been able to attract and retain some great employees by creating that purposeful experience, but also because, as our business has grown, we've been able to pay more-than-competitive salaries.

It's not only about being right; it's about getting it right and knowing that you're right. When you've been in business for thirty-three years like we have, you don't major in minor things. It's about slaying the sacred cows. We don't cling to the things that we have done well historically but just aren't working anymore and are no longer a good use of our time, money, and expertise.

THE BONUS IS RIGHT IN FRONT OF YOU

When business isn't doing well, the leader is always blamed. If Apple is down, CEO Tim Cook gets blamed. Likewise, if Northeast Private Client Group is down, Mark Murphy gets blamed. That's part of being the team leader—taking the blame and weathering the storm.

Because I fill that role for our employees and the buck stops with me when things aren't going well, I ask my team to earn their requests for increased pay and bonuses. For example, say a member of my team had seven things to do today. He did six of them perfectly, but failed on the seventh task. Well, that seventh task is where all the profit is. That's what pays for the bonuses.

When it comes to bonuses and promotions, the best businesses I've seen are crystal clear with their teams. For many years, I worked with a major international accounting firm. They had very straight-forward criteria for what was required to become a partner: have a significant book of business; be known for an area of expertise both within the firm and outside of it; be involved in committees and making the corporate culture better; and be someone with presence who management would be proud to introduce as their partner.

Employees want to know how their performance is going to be judged. I make sure my employees know exactly what they need to do to add value and keep moving up.

That way, there's no need for my employees to look to me for their bonus. The bonus is right there. The pay increase is right there. People want to blame the guy in the corner office, but I make the argument that we've given them the tools and the opportunity to continue to grow their income. I don't want those employees looking at me to hand them a bonus. I want to turn the mirror right back on them and ask, "What have you done? You had that opportunity. Did you execute?" It takes a while, but great employees will get this and respond.

The people who pick up on this concept are the ones you want to help grow your business. Those folks are going to be in the trenches with you because they want to keep getting better.

CHAPTER 5

Invest In ...Your Culture

Anyone can seek the goal of financial freedom. When a person moves from the accumulation phase of their financial life to retirement and the distribution phase, we want them to have that financial freedom. One aspect of attaining financial freedom—investing in your culture—is not a universal one. It is unique to the entrepreneur and the entrepreneurial-thinking person; that is, business owners, of course, but also executives and team leaders. If you're in a corporate environment and have employees who report to you, having a great culture and synergy within your department will add to your success, resulting in a potential promotion or you becoming more valuable to an outside corporation that wants to lure you away for more money. If you set your culture and know what you stand for, you have a formula for growing your business exponentially.

One of my most important business coaches, Dan Sullivan, whom I have worked with periodically over the past twenty-five years and am currently working with as this book goes to press, has given me much of the inspiration for writing this book. His concepts and ideas are present throughout—none more than in this chapter, as I talk about investing in your culture.

A TRANSFORMATIONAL COMPANY

Every company is experiencing one of the following:

1. **Failure:** You're just not succeeding at what you're doing.

2. **Frustration:** People around you are doing well but you don't know how to get there.

3. **Conventional success:** One's success is determined by other people's measuring sticks.

4. **Being a transformational company:** Everything is clicking on all cylinders; your competitors want to work with you or join you.

A transformational company is not only the kind of company I want to run; it's what we aspire to create for other businesses. We want them to have no competition, so they're way out in front.

Smaller entrepreneurs build a culture that revolves around them and their unique ability. They basically build their company's culture around themselves and their skill set. But there are only so many hours in the day and only so many things you can do, whereas there's almost no limit to what you can do if you've got a team of people around you who have the right culture. Understanding the importance of building a team, and making that team unstoppable through culture and synergy, is often completely overlooked in the entrepreneurial world.

> **There's almost no limit to what you can do if you've got a team of people around you who have the right culture.**

An unstoppable team has everybody on the same page using the same transformational language. A force of one is a small entrepreneur singing from his or her own songbook on culture. That business will grow arithmetically, not exponentially. Mark Cuban calls these folks "wantrepreneurs," and I'd guess that 90 to 95 percent of people who say they are entrepreneurs are not. They bought themselves a job. If you look at their companies, they have not created that culture of excellence, that culture of business development, that culture of doing whatever it takes. They're wantrepreneurs.

If you're going to grow a real business, you've got to make sure that you treat your people as well as you treat your clients. When you treat your team with that level of care and respect, you can access the secret to growing a real business: creating a culture-aware environment, a culture of business development, and a culture where your people can use your transformational language to get a predictable result every time.

CREATING A CONSISTENT CLIENT EXPERIENCE

You shouldn't expect people in your organization to be exactly as good as you, the entrepreneur, are. But you want to aspire to have a company that has a common language so the client experience is consistent. McDonald's offers the same fries in California, Kansas, and New York. It doesn't make sense if an entrepreneur having one set of discussions with a client gets different answers every time that client talks to other people in the organization. It doesn't feel like the same place with the same culture.

When everybody is singing from the same hymnal, it creates not only momentum and synergy within the organization, but also makes every client feel comfortable and confident that you have an organization that has its act together and is working in the client's best interest. You can never have that quantum leap ahead in your organization until you create that culture.

I've said that the company owner must demonstrate what a great job looks like. If employees don't get that, they must transition them out of the organization. Both are vital to maintaining your culture. When people aren't willing to put in that effort or aren't able to execute or don't play by the organization's rules, they can't stay, because they prevent you from creating that unstoppable team and that culture of excellence.

With a great culture, you have a synergistic organization that can be turbocharged—where one plus one equals three. It's the direct opposite when you have people who don't get it. They're almost like a cancer, slowly eating away at your organization's culture, or maybe even keeping your culture from being created in the first place.

DO YOU HAVE CLIENTS OR CUSTOMERS?

When you first start your business, you want every client. When I started, I tried to get an appointment with anyone and everyone. Today, as an organization, prospecting for new business involves identifying clients who are like-minded. Going after people who are not like-minded has two negative outcomes: they become customers instead of clients, and it takes a much bigger investment of time and energy to service customers.

When I was younger, I spent a lot of time trying to convince people that they should be in a relationship with us. Now, I look for people who want to be in a relationship with us and I consider whether they are going to be responsive, open-minded, and aspirational, and whether they want to transform to the life and business of their dreams. When we get a chance to work with a client like that, that's our sweet spot. We're not looking for clients who just want somebody who can buy some stocks, bonds, and insurance for them or sell them some financial products. Those people become customers.

We spend a lot of time trying to attract people who are like-minded, and we create a culture around serving them. Clients become friends and confidants. Our relationships with them energize the entire team.

Customers do the exact opposite: They suck all the energy out of the team. Customers become counterproductive in the long term. They may be doing business with you, but they suck the life out of your organization. In order to preserve the culture, it's better to step away from those customers. Ultimately, whatever revenue they bring in will always cost you more in time and effort, and serving them will chip away at the culture of your organization.

It took me a while in the business to understand how the culture needed to be spread throughout the organization. One of the revelations I had later in my career was that I was acting like Don Quixote, a solitary man on a mission. I was out there fighting and slaying the dragons. By any measure, I was successful, and many of our clients were too. But the business went from arithmetical growth to exponential growth once we developed a culture that took what I did and moved it down throughout organization.

Entrepreneurs spend so much time dealing with what's in front of us—the next meeting, the next client. Over three decades, it has become clear to me how important it is for me to schedule time to work on the culture of my business. I dedicate one day a week to it, in fact. Not one full day, but I make sure I'm working on the culture of my business throughout the week. I could fill my schedule up ten times over with existing and new clients, but dedicating that time to culture is worth it. To me, as a CEO, that's the magic elixir.

As an employer, one of the frustrations I've had over the years is dealing with employees who were good people but just didn't fit our culture. I liked them and they did a nice job, and in any other organization they would have been valued. But they wanted to become, in essence, soloists in a symphony orchestra. To create a synergistic culture, people cannot just be doing their own thing. That doesn't mean there's no room for creativity and flexibility. Everybody should be able to work in their unique skill set, and you need people with different skills, but they must be harnessed in a way that creates that "wow" experience for the clients. And it must be a repeatable process, so that everybody can do it every time. If you've managed that, you've got an organization that can really take off.

CONVERSATIONS DISAPPEAR

Good leaders create good followers. Great leaders create other great leaders. Most entrepreneurs are not great managers, but we don't need them to be great managers. For the most part, that's not what their best use is. We want them to become great leaders who fill their organizations with other people who also have leadership skills.

> **Good leaders create good followers. Great leaders create other great leaders.**

Another revelation for me was understanding the importance of continuing to reinforce and train and bring your team along. One of the buzz phrases we have in our organization is "Conversations disappear." Common thinking holds that when I put something out there— i.e., I've told someone this is how we do this, or this is what my core principles are—I should assume that that person is going to internalize it and do it that way for the rest of their life in exactly the way I told them.

Of course, it never works that way—conversations disappear. You must continue to coach and reinforce the messages until you are not the only one creating that culture. Now you have a team creating it.

Conversations disappear with clients, too, allowing them to forget the great things you've done for them. They don't consciously ignore what was said, of course; they just move ahead with their lives and the conversation fades. To counter this, we try to reinforce, in a subtle way, what we've done for clients in the past. This shows them that what we're doing for them today builds on what we've done for them in the past and leads toward a clearly articulated future.

CONVERSATIONS STILL MATTER

Just because conversations disappear does not mean you stop having them. Conversations are vital. You want an organization that really gets to know its clients and builds those relationships. You spend time finding out what the critical life events are for them, both in their business lives and their personal lives.

Relationships still count. While corporations do a lot of things well (growth, structure, and capitalization, for example), there are also things they don't do so well—in particular, maintaining personal, face-to-face relationships. My firm aspires to be an "anti-corporate corporation," meaning we leverage the things that work in corporate America without losing track of what matters most: people and relationships. Maya Angelou summed it up: "People will forget what you said, people will forget what you did, but people will never forget how you made them feel." I might be old-fashioned, but I still believe that relationships count for something.

With the goal of fostering genuine relationships, we have an organization that continually creates conversations. We do two things with those conversations.

First, we gently remind clients of the great work we've done together to reinforce why they should continue to work with us, why they should do more business with us, and why they should send everyone in their Rolodex to us because of the extraordinary work we've done together.

Then, we try to keep everyone focused on the future. I love the word *aspirational*. To quote Dan Sullivan, "Always make your future bigger than your past."[4] One of the most important lessons I've learned in life has come from seeing older clients. When they reached retirement, some had nothing to look forward to. Since they saw retirement as the end, they didn't so much die as lose interest in living. I've also seen many NFL players who retired at twenty-eight or thirty years old thinking that was the end. Our outlook for athletes is to have their second career be bigger and more successful than their playing career. We want to always orient our clients toward a future that's bigger than the past or present.

Our process makes sure that a client's life after football, or after being a CEO, is even better than the one they have today. When we're aspirational in that way, the mind-set around retirement changes. Some clients choose not to retire because they have such a passion for their business. As they age, they find a way to reinvent themselves and their role.

Entrepreneurial people don't really retire. Now, that doesn't mean

---

4   Dan Sullivan and Catherine Nomura, *The Laws of Lifetime Growth Always Make Your Future Bigger Than Your Past* (Oakland: Berrett-Koehler Publishers, 2016).

that they don't ever sell their business. They may or may not. But entrepreneurs continue having that passion for life and whatever their next venture happens to be. Our role as financial advisors is to be the vessel for that next venture. We are here to support the next great thing they'll accomplish in the middle of having a fabulous life.

You want them to choose your organization to be that vessel over the guy who is measured solely by how he does in the S&P 500. Or the guy who says, "My nephew sells insurance now, so I want to give our next piece of insurance business to him." No. Anyone can do that. You want to create an experience they can't get anywhere else. That's what your culture and your organization are trying to do—be transformational.

A CULTURE OF WINNING

During the Yankees dynasty of the late '90s, I'm not sure the Yankees were the most talented baseball team compared to the Red Sox, the Braves, and a few other teams that were competitive. Derek Jeter was the face of baseball, yet I'm not sure he was the best shortstop in the game. He was the best leader in the game, however, and there was a Yankee way. They created a culture of winning, from top to bottom.

That's what you want to create in your business—a culture of winning. Our culture is one that genuinely tries to elevate our people. We constantly point things out to help them. We do it in a way that's not critical or punitive. Our goal is to educate and inspire them so they can really understand what we're trying to do, instead of hammering them over the head with what they're doing wrong.

Our culture of winning entails clear communication. For example, we stress specificity in our client database. Instead of "in progress" or other similarly vague language to describe the status of a client's planning, our team writes something like, "We're waiting to hear from their other money manager. They've told us the expected transfer date of their assets is going to be in six business days, which will be next Wednesday. I will follow up on Friday to make sure the transfer is on track." Or, "I've been reaching out to so-and-so to get his insurance exam scheduled and he's not been responsive. I'm going to try again this week. If he doesn't respond again, I think I'm going to need Mark to get on the phone and speak with him."

It's just easier to do it right the first time. Cheap is always more expensive in the long term. Cutting corners always adds more problems. In some organizations, people do things five or six times over the course of a couple months in order to get it right. We make the effort to get it right the first time. Once you do that, then you can start to create real momentum and growth.

You create a culture in your organization in which things must be done a certain way. I learned this lesson early. In 1985, before I owned the business, there was a woman named Jane Pindar on our administrative staff. At the time, I would submit applications for securities or insurance or whatever other financial product I had sold. These were long and detailed applications, and I wasn't always as thorough as I needed to be. If there was even one blank line, Jane would circle it in red and put it back in my mailbox. She would not process it until it was 100 percent done. It didn't take me long to figure out that if I turned in anything that was not 100 percent complete, I didn't get paid.

When you create a culture of doing things a certain way in your organization, you foster efficiency and synergy—and a culture of winning.

CHAPTER 6

Invest In ...
a Second Company

Many business owners work extremely hard and put in long hours to grow 5 or 10 percent a year. Whatever organic growth is possible for any business, we've found this growth pales in comparison to what can be achieved through mergers and acquisitions. Investing in a second company through M&A, when done properly, is one of the most efficient and powerful ways to create extraordinary wealth.

If you buy a competitor, or just another business like yours, you can turbocharge your profitability—not 5, 10, or 15 percent, but 50, 100, 200, even 300 percent. All the fixed overhead is covered, so that second company becomes enormously profitable. Folded into your business, it's much more valuable than as a standalone company.

Say you have a million-dollar business that generates $200,000 a year in profits. You buy a similar business also doing $1 million and merge it into your company. Now, these two companies are running together through efficiencies and economies of scale. The first company saves $300,000 a year in expenses because of those efficiencies and economies of scale, so expenses are no longer $800,000 a year—they're $500,000. You've now taken your profitability from $200,000 a year on your first company to $500,000 on your second. Income grew from $200,000 to $700,000, a 350 percent increase.

Owners are often so busy fighting the daily battles that they can lose the strategic focus of their business. They have companies that are totally dependent on them, and they're trading their time for dollars. That's not the sign of an entrepreneurial company; it's a sign that somebody has bought themselves a job. If you really want to say you're a business owner and an entrepreneur, your business cannot be wholly dependent on your talent to perform every day.

> **If you really want to say you're a business owner and an entrepreneur, your business cannot be wholly dependent on your talent to perform every day.**

If I take a six-month sabbatical from my company and our numbers plummet, I don't have a business. Instead, I've built a company around my talents, and it's wholly dependent on my talents to perform. If that's the case, I need to invest in my business, my team, and my culture in order to build an organization that's not dependent on me, a team that works together with synergy. Having that kind of company is a prerequisite for M&A.

EARN-OUTS AND CASH WALKAWAY SALES

Most M&A deals are earn-outs. Sometimes there's cash up front, sometimes there's not. We like earn-outs because the owner of the selling company is incentivized to make sure that all the business comes over and it's profitable. Usually the seller makes something on the front end, but the majority of the money is under earn-out based on profitability.

We've also had clients with the ability to borrow money who really understood their business and their industry. An M&A opportunity came along, and they said, "This is something I want to buy. We'll do a cash walkaway sale." With a cash walkaway sale, you have to do your due diligence and know your business, because you're at risk when you borrow money. The more money you borrow from the bank, the more things you *hope* to have happen will *have to* happen.

COMPANIES MAY SEARCH YOU OUT

To be clear, businesses should still do all they can to grow organically. But you should always be out there exploring opportunities to buy your competitors, because the potential for growth from M&A is much greater than what you can get through organic internal growth.

A company may become available for purchase because it's poorly run, because someone would like to slow down or retire, or because of a change in life circumstances for the owner. If you're running a company that is transformational in your space, you may not have to search out your competitors to buy them. They may search you out to become part of your company.

Since the introduction of free agency in the NFL, some of the best players in the league have sought out the New England Patriots because they've been an iconic football team for fifteen seasons. Players want to be part of the Patriots way. They'll even do it at a steep discount because they get to be part of that culture and have a chance to win a Super Bowl. If you can create a company that has that kind of culture, excitement, and leadership, you may find your competitors seeking you out. Then you know you're on the right track.

In my own business, it's validation for me when some of the most successful people in my industry search me out. Some are looking for me to help them with their business; others want to work together. Not only do they see our firm benefiting clients, they also see an opportunity to grow their experience, their income, and their lives because of efficiencies and economies of scale.

Properly executed M&A transactions are done with synergy. It takes expertise in this space to put together these kinds of deals. There are many, many examples of mergers and acquisitions that have failed because they were done improperly or under the wrong circumstances.

TAKE A PAGE FROM WALL STREET'S BOOK

M&A is one of the biggest drivers of higher stock prices. When Company A buys Company B and they can run those two companies together, earnings go up, the company grows, and stock prices rise. There has been example after example after example of this over the last hundred years on Wall Street. Companies grow their value and the value of their stock not necessarily through day-to-day operations, but with their ability to play the M&A game.

The same principles apply to small and mid-sized companies— it's just that most smaller companies don't have the vision or foresight to successfully follow through on M&A. In principle, though, these deals are all the same.

With M&A, there is always an integration period. But think about the amount of work it takes to grow your company organically 5 or 10 percent. Would you like to grow your company 50 percent this year? Would you like to triple your growth over the next five years? To do that organically is extremely difficult. How much easier would it be to bring all the business and all the clients over in one fell swoop?

THE TRANSITION: HIT THE GROUND RUNNING

In preparation for an M&A transaction, you've got to gear up for a seamless transition so that you hit the ground running on all cylinders. During the transition, you're making sure you get a disproportionate share of customers over into your business. You're making sure there's great communication between the new employees and your existing employees, whom you've prepared for what's happening and what to expect. You need to be radically transparent so everybody knows the endgame. It can't be just the C-suite or corner office that understands the strategy—everybody on the team needs to understand what you're trying to do.

The core principle we use during the transition is economies of scale. If you drive more revenue through the same overhead, you will have a more profitable business. The secondary principle is turbocharging that newly bought or merged company. Size gives you different opportunities. With a larger company, it might be possible to buy employee benefits at a lower rate. Your purchasing power has gone up, so you can negotiate a lower rate with vendors. You get better deals from your suppliers. In certain industries, an M&A deal might create scarcity—meaning you may be taking a competitor out of the marketplace, which allows you to raise your prices.

It's always industry-specific. Not all the tools work all the time. Maybe you won't be able to raise your prices. Maybe you've got mostly union employees and a union-negotiated contract, so you won't be able to negotiate benefits. It's very individual. But there are always opportunities to turbocharge once you're taking advantage of economies of scale—when you've taken two companies and are generating more revenue through the same (or lower) fixed overhead.

ONE PLUS ONE EQUALS THREE—EVEN DURING A RECESSION

The world is looking for one plus one equals two. The result is often one plus one equals one and a half. We want one plus one equals three. We encourage all our clients who are business owners to ask if there is an opportunity to buy one of their competitors. This opportunity is sometimes even greater when the economy is down.

I've done many deals during tough economic times. A once profitable company begins to struggle when a recession hits, and we're often able to buy that company for next to nothing. We give the employees jobs and give the owner a five-year contract, and we are able to drive more revenue through our business without adding costs.

When the economy is good, companies may not be in the selling mind-set. But when the economy gets tough, cash flow gets tight, capitalization is low, and people panic. If a company is well-run and does not panic during a recession, it can be in a position to buy its struggling competitors, sometimes for pennies on the dollar. Some of our clients had their most prolific growth during the last recession.

BE A TRANSFORMATIVE COMPANY

In order to be able to fully take advantage of M&A opportunities, you want to be a company that is transformative in your industry. To be that kind of company, you still want to focus on all the markers of organic growth and running a great business. You want to do what the first half of this book is about: investing in yourself, your business, your people, and your culture. It goes back to the concept of *be, do, have* from chapter 3. You have to *be* a company that's transformative and *do* that work. Only then will you *have* people seeking you out to do business with you.

I talk with my employees every day about how there are a lot of people licensed to sell the products and services that we offer. Why is somebody going to choose our company over another? Why are our existing customers going to choose to stay with us? What makes us different? If you can't answer those questions, then your business is in jeopardy of being commoditized. If you can't tell me about your niche and what your value proposition is, or why we should work with your company over everybody else, that's a sign that your business is vulnerable.

If I can get the same thing somewhere else, what happens when your competitor decides to lower their prices? What if a big competitor comes into the marketplace and prices their products below yours? What happens if the inevitable increase in expenses happens on that side of the ledger, and because you've become commoditized you're not able to raise your prices to keep up with your costs? You may not go out of business, but your profitability will get lower and lower. That's happening in many industries today with consolidation and commoditization. If people can't transform their companies in this climate, those companies get commoditized and slowly bleed to death.

Some companies are vulnerable. Others are poised to take

advantage of changes in the marketplace. The companies that are nimble and adaptive can not only win the day, but become much more profitable than they were before.

AFTER M&A: WHAT TO DO WITH INCREASED PROFITABILITY

Enhanced profitability gives the entrepreneur the opportunity to create much more personal wealth. It also provides the cash flow necessary to make reinvestments in the businesses in order to compete in the future. The money you generate through a properly executed M&A deal allows you to reinvest in your business with a lot less risk because you're doing it out of cash flow rather than borrowing. Now there's money to do renovations, buy inventory (at a much lower price because you're buying by the container-load rather than by the truckload), and hire talented employees.

Being transformative and profitable is important for a business's ability to attract top talent. How are you going to have mediocre talent around you and run a great company? Now that you have a more profitable business and increased cash flow, you will be able to get the best and brightest to come work for you. But in order to attract that kind of talent, you must have a business that's worthy.

HOW YOUR EMPLOYEES BENEFIT

If you're employed by a company that's more profitable because they've acquired, sold, or merged and taken advantage of economies of scale, then you have greater job security. More profitable companies have the ability to pay their employees more. Many are able to offer employees better opportunities for training and advancement. New career opportunities arise because there are new roles to fill when two companies are integrated.

Even if you're not a business owner, understanding the principles of M&A may inspire you get on the entrepreneurial side of the equation. During the integration of two companies, M&A creates opportunities for existing employees to run a division of the other company. If you're number two in sales, you might be able to run the sales division in the company you just bought, and move up to the number one person in that division.

When we have a good year at my company, I don't keep all the extra profits. Many companies have bonus plans, and if you double your profitability the bonus pool also doubles. Employees are rewarded. In my company I look at the net profitability of the business at the end of the year, and that gets shared with our team. With M&A, there's something in it for everybody.

CHAPTER 7

Invest In ... Real Estate

Real estate is underutilized as a class of assets. We believe in Financial Balance®, and real estate is an asset that works in most people's portfolios. Our experience working with entrepreneurial folks is that the people who have created tremendous amounts of wealth have created a company that produces cash flow, and they've taken that cash flow and invested it in income-producing real estate.

One of the tenets of our financial planning is creating a series of assets that produces either a guaranteed or highly reliable stream of income. When clients decide to retire and their earned income stops, that stream of income starts. Real estate is one of the top asset classes to provide that stream of income.

LOCATION, LOCATION, LOCATION

Real estate works as a top asset class because, over time, valuable properties tend to appreciate. Historically, real estate in the right location rises in value. If you find the right desirable piece of property, over the long term its value will appreciate.

It's also an asset that produces income because either your business or another entity is paying rent on that property. On top of that, real estate is a leverageable asset. Making the down payment may be the last time you put any money into that piece of property. The rent pays the mortgage and taxes. If it's a commercial lease, then it's a triple net lease, meaning the tenant pays the taxes and insurance. Eventually, over a series of years, that mortgage will get paid off and you'll have a free and clear property.

Real estate in the right location does four things:

1. It provides an asset that, historically, increases in value over time.

2. It allows for a mortgage on the property that gets paid by somebody else's dollars.

3. It produces income for you.

4. It allows an investor to take advantage of favorable tax laws.

TAX ADVANTAGES

There are a lot of tax benefits to having real estate. The biggest one is depreciation, which allows you to write off the property over a period of time and reduce the federal income tax you pay.

Real estate is a tax-advantaged asset. You never have to sell real estate during your lifetime, yet there are many ways to access your money in a tax-efficient manner. As you develop more equity in the property and the mortgage goes down, you can refinance the property and pull out cash on a tax-free basis.

If you do decide to sell, that also has tax benefits. When you sell, you don't pay ordinary income tax like you would on a 401(k) or an

IRA; you pay capital gains tax, which is a much lower rate. What's more, the government allows you to do a 1031 exchange. Instead of selling the property and paying tax on it, you can sell the property and move that money to another piece of real estate—a like-kind, tax-free exchange.

INCOME PRODUCTION

We don't recommend our clients put all their money in any one place, but income-producing real estate has shown time and time again to be an asset that produces regular and predictable income.

Let's say you have a commercial property that has a long-term, triple net lease on it. The tenant pays taxes and insurance; if either goes up it's the tenant's responsibility. The landlord is going to get their rent monthly on that ten- or fifteen-year lease. Generally, there are escalations in those leases, so that landlord will have an ever-increasing stream of income.

Compare that scenario to putting a similar amount of money into the stock market. You're pulling down a steady stream of income, right? But then the market has a 40 percent hiccup. Now, instead of pulling down a steady stream of income, you have to grossly reduce what you're taking out of the market until it recovers—or you see your capital depreciate. If you continue pulling out money, you're now taking a much higher percentage from your portfolio (which has a significantly lower value following the hiccup).

Real estate works as long as you don't get overleveraged—meaning you're buying too much property and have more debt than you can handle. You must be in a position where if that piece of property is vacant for a period it's not going to collapse the rest of your empire.

I go back to the theory that even too much broccoli can kill you. Real estate is terrific, but too much overleveraged real estate can kill you as well.

AN ASSET UNDERUSED BY THE MASSES

Real estate is an asset that remains underutilized by most people. It's also an asset used during tough economic times to create a lot of wealth. During a market downturn, some of our wealthiest clients heavily invested in real estate are not overwhelmed. Even when real estate is in a downward cycle, our clients who own a lot of real estate are not bothered. They have enough capital, and they aren't selling. They know those leases are likely to come in.

They also know that, historically, real estate goes up over time. Knowing that they have liquidity, they're waiting for people to panic. Then prices to go down, and they get a great sale. That's when money is made. There is money made during good times as well, but where the tremendous amounts of money are made is when you have a downward economic cycle in real estate and you're someone with enough liquidity and the ability to borrow from a bank. That's where people are making killings in the real estate market.

Of course, people are also making money during good economic times. When you're buying high-quality pieces of property, there's much more going on behind the scenes than just your rate of return. A client who runs through their mortgage and rent might be getting 2–6 percent on their money. What's the big deal about that? Well, it's not the rate of return that's the big deal; what's going on behind the scenes is the big deal. That property is appreciating. That mortgage is getting paid off and you'll have a free and clear property. The rent will increase over time.

A STRONG, STEADY, AND SOLID LONG-TERM ASSET

Our entrepreneurial clients who are smart are making more money than they're consuming. They're net savers, and they don't need money currently.

When clients do need money, however, real estate can provide that income. Real estate becomes a long-term asset that is strong, steady, and solid. Once the mortgage gets paid off, property values and rent rise, and our client gets closer to retirement, that property becomes a highly reliable stream of income.

Our successful clients get to the point where they have enough income from different assets that they're never worried where that paycheck is coming from. They're not worried about being able to do the things they want to do in their life. Real estate is an asset that can provide that kind of security.

Ultimately, real estate can become a multigenerational asset. It helps create wealth long-term for the original owner of that property, but it can be a dynastic asset that will help create wealth for their kids and their kids' kids.

And while the long-term benefits are potentially multigenerational for the smart investor, with real estate you make your money not on the sell but on the buy. If you buy correctly, you can make a fair amount of money quickly. It depends on how much you put down on the property; with most properties, most of the money is spent paying down the mortgage, not the down payment. In a properly structured deal, that property will produce some positive cash flow right away.

FIRST LEVEL FOR BUSINESS OWNERS

When we do an analysis for our clients who own businesses, the first level of real estate to pursue is buying the space where their office is located. If you think you can predictably use that space—it's not too big or too small; it's a good place to house your business for the long haul—it's instructive to analyze how much rent you would pay to a landlord over the next thirty or forty years.

If you own a business for ten, twenty, thirty, forty years, and you rent your office space, at the end of that time you'll have no asset. You will have used that property to house your business, but you won't have any equity in the property. If you own the building, instead, you'll have a free and clear property that will be there to produce income for you in retirement, create wealth for the next generation, or be a sellable asset. With a 1031 exchange, you can sell that property, reinvest the proceeds in another property, and defer all capital gains taxes.

For many of our clients in high-profile locations, over the long-term the investment in their business's office space actually becomes more profitable than the business itself—and these are folks who have very successful businesses. It's not uncommon for us to have a client who grows their business for twenty years and sells it for $2 million or $3 million, but they sell the building they're in for $6 million or $7 million. Again, location is critical. (That scenario is possible in areas where real estate accelerates, like New York, New Jersey, and California. In rural areas of the Midwest, real estate does not appreciate at the level it does on the coasts.)

YOUR RISKS AND YOUR TEAM

You must put together a strong team around you and have enough liquidity and/or borrowing power. Therefore, a market drop won't take down the property, much less other areas of your wealth. You need great people around you who can help you maintain your property. Your team should include a great banker, a great real estate attorney, a great financial advisor, and a great leasing agent to find you tenants.

Real estate has cycles just like every other asset. It doesn't just go in one direction. During an economic downturn, you might be in between tenants for an extended period. When something goes wrong with the building, you need to have either enough liquidity or the borrowing ability to survive that storm and right the ship. You need to have knowledge about those scenarios and surround yourself with sharp professionals who can help you navigate those waters safely and effectively.

DON'T TRY THIS AT HOME

With everyone's face buried in their phone, we all have access to a lot of information. What the internet does not provide is access to wisdom. Many smart people believe they can be their own financial advisor; they believe they can be their own key business strategist and critical thinker. The internet told them to do this and not do that.

But often you get conflicting advice from online searches. One blog says do one thing; another says *never* do that thing. There is so much bad information out there masking as financial advice.

Perhaps the only area where there's more bad advice is around dieting. If all these diet books and blogs were successful, everyone would be skinny, right? If all these financial books and blogs worked so well, everybody would be financially stable, right? Yet most people are not able to retire and keep the lifestyle they want. If they decide to be their own financial self-help guru, they'll end up working far longer than they wanted to work.

You don't want to try any of this on your own. You want to be part of a team—you've got to surround yourself with knowledge-able professionals. You're the quarterback of that team. People who have been successful in business who decide from ego (because they're smart and successful) that they can be their own financial advisor have a low chance of success. They *could* get lucky on their own, but it rarely happens. They end up working many more years than they wanted to work and not having the lifestyle they want.

If you had a heart problem today, would you want me, with my finance degree, to handle your surgery? To me, people's belief in their own intellect and ability to absorb information and act wisely as their own financial advisor is no different than me, with a finance background, doing cardiac surgery on a client because I read on the internet how to do cardiac surgery.

HAVE I DEVELOPED A PLAN?

Whether you're an employee or business owner, real estate can be a part of your long-term plan. Ask yourself, "Have I developed a plan where, at some point, whether it be normal retirement age or even earlier, I have enough guaranteed or highly reliable streams of income to replace my paycheck so I can stay home and have the same lifestyle?" For most Americans, the answer is no. They don't have the right financial advisor, they don't have the right plan, and they don't have the right discipline.

If we can help you find the right piece of real estate—a desirable place that tenants will want to rent—coupled with the fact that the government gives you significant tax benefits, it's a great investment. As inflation goes up, the price of your property goes up. If you buy that property with the right team advising you and you handle it correctly, you'll wake up in ten, twenty, or thirty years and have an asset that is in a position to replace a chunk of income and be one of the pillars of your retirement plan.

The main case for real estate is that it will remain an asset class that works. The best time to plant a tree was twenty years ago. The next best time is today. You're never too late to invest in real estate.

CHAPTER 8

Invest In ...
Financing Deals

Mark Cuban believes that most people who think they're entrepreneurs are not. It's true. Most people who own their own business and say they're entrepreneurs are not. They *bought* themselves a job. They're trading time for dollars, and their business only operates if they get up very early, work very hard, and stay very late. It's not five days per week either—it's seven. These folks become prisoners to their business.

"Wantrepreneurs" get paid on what they do, not on what they own. To cure that problem, we figure out how to create money while we're asleep. How do we have income coming in all the time, even when we're not actually working? It's understandable that business owners, before becoming real entrepreneurs, trade time for dollars. They need money to pay the bills and the mortgage, send the kids to college, and maintain their lifestyle.

The core idea behind financing deals is putting your capital to work, not your efforts. Most of our clients make their money through owning a business or running another operating company. Investors are getting outsized returns when they finance deals that are successful. Being on the lending side of the transaction is incredibly attractive to smart investors who have done their due diligence.

These types of assets are attractive not only because of the high rates of return, but also because that return is created largely without your day-to-day efforts. Further, there are tax benefits. Investments in operating companies are tax-deductible, and many things can be expensed.

When you finance deals, this is done with your money and other people's time and effort. It's a game-changer when done properly. Tremendous amounts of wealth can be created. However, tremendous amounts of wealth can also be lost. These deals are high risk, high reward.

NOT FOR THE FAINT OF HEART

The reason the returns are so outsized is because of the risk involved. Financing deals can be very sophisticated work with a tremendous amount of risk—not something that anyone should be doing without a great deal of due diligence. These deals aren't for the faint of heart.

There are also barriers to entry. These prerequisites determine if you are a big enough player to get involved. You must be an accredited investor to participate. This generally means having a high income and net worth. You must sign what I call "big boy paperwork" or "big girl paperwork," which absolves the person you're investing with of liability for virtually everything but fraud or theft.

There is also significant risk in relying on somebody else to run the day-to-day operations. You're making the investment and trusting that that person's daily efforts will make the company successful. But you're one level removed from being able to control the process. In my business, when things have gotten tough over the last thirty years, I could put in fourteen-hour days, or eighteen-hour days, and right the ship. You don't have that ability when you're relying on other people.

Furthermore, if you make one of these investments, you take full responsibility, which means accepting all the glory for a great investment and all the blame for one that doesn't work. You must be prepared to lose 100 percent of your money and blame no one but yourself.

You have to know yourself to get involved on the lending side of the equation. Can you afford, both financially and emotionally, to lose that investment? If you want total safety,

> **You must be prepared to lose 100 percent of your money and blame no one but yourself.**

put your money in Treasury bills, an insured bank account, or whole life insurance policies. Put it in an asset that never has a bad day.

But if you're looking to create a lot of wealth, financing deals can become the way to do that. It takes three different forms: lending to someone who can't get bank financing; investing in an existing operating company; or being involved in starting an operating company.

LENDING TO PEOPLE WHO CAN'T GET A BANK LOAN

First, we're seeing a great deal of wealth created by clients who decide to lend money to people who are good credit risks. These folks have businesses with assets behind them and plenty of collateral. But they also have some characteristic in their profile that does not allow them to go to a bank for traditional financing.

For example, we've seen clients do business with contractors who don't show a lot of income on the books. Their income is up and down, and their credit is not great. But they have a great piece of property and are renovating a house to flip. Say it's a $1 million house that's free and clear; they'll need another $500,000 to finish the renovation. Once that renovation is complete, the house is going to be worth over $2 million.

There's plenty of equity in that scenario. Even if the contractor screws up, you still have $1 million of collateral. But the bank won't lend that contractor the money. There are many, many reasons why a traditional bank wouldn't be interested. Some part of that contractor's profile makes them not a candidate for traditional financing. Often, it's that their credit or income isn't good.

That contractor should be able to explain to you why they need the money and show you why your investment will be secure. Then, if you lend the money to finance that contractor's operation—they borrow money from you for a year—you've made a reasonably secure investment that will allow them to finish the house and pay you back with interest. We've seen deals where the loan was repaid at 10, 12, 15, or 18 percent. Sometimes, the deal stipulates that a percentage of profits on the sale go to the investor as well.

This type of lending ties up money in a reasonably secure way that can get a much higher rate of return than traditional investments. Yet the risk is still significant. That contractor is willing to pay high-percentage interest because they can't get money from a bank. If they were bankable, they'd get a loan at 4 or 5 percent. If that company was such a sure shot, it would be financed internally by the founders. They wouldn't need to go for outside capital. There is always risk when you're financing a deal for someone who can't get a bank loan.

LENDING TO OPERATING COMPANIES

The second way to finance deals is through a pure private equity play. Ultimately, this creates the opportunity to get a much higher than average—if not huge—return on your money.

With this kind of deal, you're looking for a well-run operating company that has a great business idea at its core. You could shoot for a company that will go public; you could make ten, twenty, or thirty times returns on your money. More often, a private equity play targets a company that is going to be in business for a long time, be profitable, and pay great dividends. Ideally, you're able to figure out the exit strategy for that operating company, whether it's going public, being bought out, or being bought up by another company.

There are many reasons why you would choose one operating company over another. Often, it's an industry where you have some knowledge. Of course, it must also be about the people. We believe that you don't invest in companies, you invest in people. Investing in people you trust and admire, and who have a track record of success, is vital.

> Investing in people you trust and admire, and who have a track record of success, is vital.

This type of deal is at the top of your risk pyramid. If you believe in Financial Balance® and you want to fill up all the buckets, this is the bucket at the top of the pyramid with the greatest risk. These investments are speculative; that means this is a high-risk, high-reward asset. If everybody could get ten, twenty, or thirty times on their money without any risk, everybody would be doing these deals. Whatever amount of money you're prepared to put into a private equity play, you must be prepared to lose all of your investment. Even the very best private equity firms have more losers than winners.

You can't succumb to fear of missing out, or FOMO. A lot of people get greedy. They have FOMO, so they invest money not earmarked for this kind of risk. That can really set their financial world back dramatically. Tragedies happen when someone takes non-discretionary money unintended for this kind of investment and chooses to finance a deal with it. They use their mortgage money or kids' college money. Unfortunately, we see people do this all the time because of greed and fear of missing out.

LENDING TO START AN OPERATING COMPANY

The third way to get involved in financing deals is to help start an operating company that you're not 100 percent the owner of and are not going to run day to day. You're going to make money from other people's efforts.

An example of starting an operating company in an industry you know and have done your due diligence is an investment I made in a company called OraCare. They make a deoxychloride mouthwash. I'm a co-founder and member of the board. Of course, I'm not saying you should or should not invest in a similar company. This is merely an example of an area where I did my due diligence and found an attractive investment.

It's up to every investor to do their own research and make the decision for themselves. For decades, I've been advising dentists on how to create wealth and run better practices, so I understand their business. OraCare was put together by a group of dentists with an acute understanding of why this product would be become the standard of care in dentistry. They saw that this was something needed in their industry. On top of that, they had contacts to be able to market the product. They not only had knowledge that it was the right product, they had the ability to distribute that knowledge and get a critical mass going with just the people in their network. OraCare is only a few years old, but it's already become profitable.

Again, it comes back to the people. Only finance a deal for someone you respect. For instance, you could finance one of the junior partners in your firm who is ready to open their own company. You want to be their partner, or they want you to be their partner. They need your money, of course, but they also want your expertise and sound guidance.

DUE DILIGENCE

By financing deals, you'll uncover the potential to create tremendous amounts of wealth. But it's also where fortunes are lost. You must thoroughly investigate an operating company in which to invest; you must proceed extremely carefully.

About every other week a marijuana deal comes across my desk. Why? Because marijuana is now legal in many states, and it appears this trend will continue. This has created a rush for marijuana producers and related products and services. A handful of those businesses will do extremely well. A few will make a lot of money and be very successful. Most, however, will not. Some will barely make it. Many will fail. People who put money into those deals will lose 100 percent of their investment. There's just not room for thousands of marijuana companies to succeed.

Fear of missing out is powerful and can get people to make unwise investments. I keep hearing people say, "Marijuana's hot right now. I need to get in on marijuana." Well, okay, but there are thousands of marijuana companies out there. You better pick one of the few that is going to be successful in that space. If you have some discretionary money and want to take a shot, great. That's your business. But don't do it with your kid's education fund. Don't do it with money you can't afford to lose.

REGISTERED INVESTMENT ADVISORS *CANNOT* GIVE ADVICE ON FINANCING DEALS

As a registered investment advisor, I cannot give advice on operating companies in which to invest. You must do your own research, and you need outside sources to help with this. I cannot bring a deal to a client and say, "You should put your money here." Every day, somebody is asking me about a deal—a private equity deal or some other transaction they're considering. We discuss it. But that conversation always ends with me saying the same thing: "I can't give you any advice on whether you should put your money in this deal. I'm not legally allowed to do that. You have to make your own decision."

It's not much different than when a client tells me they're thinking about divorcing their husband or wife. I do a lot of listening, but, ultimately, I do not give advice on whether they should divorce their spouse. Again, the glory and the blame all falls to the investor.

PROCEED WITH EXTREME CAUTION

The reason that broker dealers and other institutions don't want their registered investment advisors making these types of recommendations is because of the risk involved. These are uncertain investments, plain and simple, so if people lose money they will be looking for somebody to sue. If somebody tells you, "You should put all your money into that," and you lose your investment, you're going to want to go after that person.

That's not how it works. You need your own sources to evaluate these deals. You've got to find outside advisors who are experts in the industry to help. Our clients who choose to finance deals generally have some background in private equity, but they also have experts around them. The mantra: "You don't invest in companies, you invest in people," is also helpful when thinking about surrounding yourself with the necessary advisors.

Most importantly, you need an attorney who specializes in deals, deal flow, and private equity. That's not every attorney out there. In fact, it's a very small group. Just like it's a very small group of investors with the discretionary money, accreditation as an investor, and the ability to do the due diligence on these types of transactions. An attorney who's an expert in this space will understand all the various investment options and make sure the contract does the best possible job of protecting your investment.

Language is important in these contracts. I learned this lesson the hard way. I've invested in deals that went down, and the contracts didn't include language to protect my money. If I had just insisted on a personal guarantee from the person on the other side of the transaction—which I probably would have gotten—even though the deal wasn't successful, they would still have to pay me since they owned a lot of other assets. But they didn't have to pay me because of the contract's wording.

* * *

Some of the largest, most successful companies were created through financing deals. Some of the greatest companies in the world were founded by someone who had an idea and another person who came up with the cash to invest. There are certainly millionaires and billionaires who have made their wealth from companies they built with only a great idea and work ethic. But along with that, you need a certain amount of time and luck.

People have had their financial lives greatly enhanced—and greatly set back—by these transactions. The moral of this chapter is not to encourage or discourage readers from financing deals. We never give advice on whether or not to get involved in private equity. We simply want to let people know that great fortunes have been made, and lost, and that financing deals requires caution, due diligence, and outside advice.

CHAPTER 9

Getting Paid as a Landlord, Practitioner, CEO, and Owner

Our most successful business owner clients get paid four ways: As a landlord and business owner, they get paid for what they own; as a practitioner and CEO, they get paid for what they do.

Many business owners are at a point where they own their office space and take home a salary for whatever role they fill within the company. That's getting paid as a landlord and practitioner. To get paid four ways, the question becomes how much you're putting into the bottom line after you pay yourself as landlord and practitioner. What's left to reinvest in the business? You need to have a certain percentage of profitability that allows you to make reinvestments, pay a CEO salary, and get dividends as an owner.

If we take you out of the business, and you can't show up for a month, six months, or a year, do you still have a business when you return? If the answer is no, you don't have a business. You've bought yourself a nice paying job at which you trade your time for dollars. In order to get paid four ways, you must build a business that's both profitable and can function without you.

LANDLORD: GETTING PAID FOR WHAT YOU OWN

If you rent an office space for twenty years, at the end of that time you're going to have the inside of a donut to show for it. And not only are you paying rent for twenty years without creating any equity, you're typically going to see a 3 to 4 percent increase in costs every year.

But if you own the building and have a fixed mortgage, you can lock in a fixed cost of rent. At the end of those twenty years, you have a free-and-clear building. You have tax benefits. And if you bought in the right area, you have capital appreciation and an asset that will have grown substantially over time.

If you don't yet own the property where your office is located, consider whether your building is a space that's going to be able to support your business for an extended period of time. If so, then all you're really doing is switching, conceptually, from rent to mortgage. You're paying rent to yourself and a mortgage to a third party.

We've had a lot of clients who were lucky enough to buy office real estate in Los Angeles, San Francisco, New York City, or another area with a highly desirable real estate market. After twenty or thirty years, not only did they have a successful business, they had real estate that was worth as much or more. That real estate became another asset for them to be able to rent or sell—i.e., a passive, income-producing asset not dependent on the owner's labor.

It's not uncommon for our clients to sell their business or part of it, and as part of the transaction create a long-term lease on the building that gives them guaranteed income in retirement. Owning your office space, provided it's in a desirable location and is the right fit for your business, doesn't have to be your first step to getting paid four ways—maybe you currently rent your space—but it should be an asset that you seriously consider along your path to creating extraordinary wealth.

PRACTITIONER: GETTING PAID FOR WHAT YOU DO

Most business owners have a job they do at their company. Of course, we want them to get paid for doing that job. Whether you're a doctor, salesperson, or CFO, you should always be getting paid for your practitioner role. Whether it's $150,000, $200,000, or $400,000 per year, we want you to get paid for the job that you do.

For example, I'm responsible for marketing our firm, growing our intellectual property, and making sure enough clients are coming through the door to fill the book of business for every advisor on my team. I take home a salary for this work, which is separate from my role and compensation as CEO.

Our firm has 3,500 total clients and 1,500 unique relationships. I'm responsible for closing and maintaining the most important relationships, generally the larger clients, and for the sources who are referring new business to our company. I'm responsible for building relationships and closing deals. Writing this book is an example of my role as practitioner: I'm working on the intellectual property of our firm and marketing our services by writing a book that will give our team a competitive advantage.

CEO: GETTING PAID FOR WHAT YOU DO

If you're just getting paid for the job that you're doing, however, you're not an entrepreneur. You have a job; you're trading your time for dollars. But you could be doing that job elsewhere and have fewer headaches because it's not your business. You'd get your paycheck, go home every night, and be done.

In my business, I'm the CEO and I'm accountable for all aspects of the business. I've got a team: a CFO, a COO, a Director of Operations, a junior partner, an executive assistant, and a driver, among many others. I've got all kinds of people who work for me, and it's my job to responsibly run the company. At the same time, I also have my practitioner role of bringing in clients and working on the firm's IP.

An entrepreneurial CEO assumes the risk, stress, obligation, and liability.

When you're a practitioner and a CEO, you're getting to the place of being a real entrepreneur. An entrepreneurial CEO assumes the risk, stress, obligation, and liability. The CEO is someone who has to be there every day and not only do their job, as a practitioner, but manage the company as well.

As CEO, I've got all the responsibility. I've got all the risk. I've got lines of credit and the liability of all my employees. I've got the overhead. I've got the stress where my phone is always on, and it could blow up at any time with a problem. If I'm not getting paid for all that, why wouldn't I just be a sales guy someplace, go home at five o'clock, and enjoy a stress-free evening with my spouse and kids? If you're shouldering the responsibility of being the CEO of your company, you should be getting paid for that. By taking that risk, stress, and obligation and liability, that's what makes you an entrepreneur. That's what helps you create wealth.

The question I ask many folks who say they're entrepreneurs is, "What happens to this business if you decide to go into the Witness Protection Program for six months or a year? Or even just one month?" That's where the rubber hits the road. Most of them tell me that the business would collapse. Well, they don't have a business then; they have a job. We don't want to create just an employment opportunity—we want to create a business.

OWNER: GETTING PAID FOR WHAT YOU OWN

Nearly every company is unique in how the owner's compensation is handed out. Sometimes, they're paid annually, sometimes quarterly, sometimes monthly. In theory, as the owner of the business, you should be able to stay home, sleep in, and guard the driveway while somebody else runs the company. That's the hallmark of whether you really have a business. You just get a check.

As the owner of that company, that business becomes more valuable as it grows. Ultimately, it can be sold to a third party or, as I'm doing now, selling it off to junior partners over time. Many family businesses have passive owners along with those who are involved in the day-to-day business. One of the children might not even know where the office is located, but he or she is getting a dividend check every year as a passive owner of that business. Another of the children actually runs the business; he or she goes to that office every day and makes all the decisions. Those two have different levels of profit.

If I've got to be worried about the business 24/7, if I'm the one who has to be there and make tough decisions, I'm going to want a higher compensation than if I just sat at home and go to the mailbox once a quarter to get my dividend check.

REINVESTING IN YOUR BUSINESS

Sometimes the owner doesn't take their dividend check but instead reinvests in the business to grow it. This year in my business, for example, we were able to find a Chief Investment Officer who was a four-star-rated Morning Star manager and had a background at Goldman Sachs. But it wasn't like when this talent became available we said, "Great, we've got room in our budget to bring in an enormous salary." When I saw that we had the ability to hire that CIO, I said, "Rather than take full dividend checks this year as owners, let's reinvest it and get this guy on our team." Our dividends were lower than they would have been, but we're already seeing the business grow with our investment in a top-notch CIO.

Or perhaps you choose to invest in technology. You're on track to take a certain dividend, but then a piece of technology comes out that you think will give a great ROI to your business, help your business grow, and help you stay ahead of your competition—and make more money in the long run. Let's say that piece of technology costs $100,000. The owners make a business decision to take $100,000 less in distributions this year as profits, believing it's going to make $200,000 a year for the rest of their lives. If an identical business to ours chooses not to make that $100,000 investment, the owners would take home another $100,000 that year, but the next year we would take home $200,000—and $200,000 again the year after that, and the year after that.

Most owners don't invest back in their business. They don't want to spend the money, so they don't make that investment that could allow them to stay ahead of their competition. Over time, a lot of those businesses get commoditized.

As an entrepreneurial owner, however, you make that choice to invest in yourself. Although I've got personal money in the stock market, bonds, insurance, real estate, and private equity, the best investments I've ever made were when I've invested in my company. What our entrepreneurial clients love about this, and what I love about it, is that when you invest in yourself, you have control. People are always worried about the stock market going down. Articles are coming out saying it's overvalued, and we know that in every cycle we see a big downturn in the market. But none of us can personally control whether the stock market goes up or down by 20 percent this year, or stays flat. But we do have control when we invest in ourselves.

What's more, I know it's a good investment because I've spent my life's work becoming an expert in my business. I've put in my "ten thousand hours" to become world-class. That doesn't mean every investment I make pays off, but I'm making calculated, thought-out risks. Although I've spent some money and lost it, if I had not taken those risks I would not have ended up creating a significant ROI for us over time.

Which is not to say that you put every penny you own into your business. Some entrepreneurs do that early in their careers. We've talked about our belief in Financial Balance®—i.e., not putting all your eggs in one basket. At some point, you want to diversify, fill up lots of buckets, and create Financial Balance®.

But I always have a bias for investing in myself. I believe that's how every entrepreneur should think. That's how our clients have created multi-generational wealth. They didn't create that level of wealth by putting it into mutual funds.

THE UNIVERSAL MARKER OF A BUSINESS

After you get paid as a landlord and pay all the rest of your expenses, and pay yourself a salary to do your day job (this is really a company expense as well), how much money is left at the end of the year for distributions and reinvestment back into the company? That's the central question that separates a real business owner from a "wantrepreneur," to use Mark Cuban's term.

It's different for every industry, and no two businesses are exactly alike. But you can use this strategy to figure out where your business is. We have a general rule of thumb around how much you should be putting to the bottom line, which then goes to distributions, reinvestments in the business, and the CEO's compensation. The percentage differs in every industry, but we like to see our clients put 20 percent to the bottom line after they've covered their expenses and been paid as landlord and practitioner.

In some industries it's lower; others, it's a lot higher. Whatever the industry, if they're able to put a solid percentage of revenue to the bottom line after getting paid as landlord and practitioner, then they've got a business. They haven't just bought themselves a nice paying job.

Earlier, I joked that a business owner can sleep late and guard the driveway, but as that kind of business owner you're taking on enormous responsibility. You're always at risk of everything ending. And that means it not only ends for you and your family, but for your clients, who may or may not find other people to work with, and for your staff, whom you've provided jobs to support their families. The owner deserves to be compensated for shouldering that risk.

CAPABILITY AND PROFITABILITY

Getting paid as CEO, in addition to your role as practitioner, is the most challenging of the four, because you must be putting a certain amount of money to the bottom line. How do you build that capability into your business and have that level of profitability? How do you create something that goes beyond meeting the day-to-day needs of the business and starts creating real wealth? You change the dynamics of your business, but it won't happen right away. Often, it takes years to get that done.

It did for me. For many years, I built the business around my ability to sell and be a good financial advisor. In other words, I built it around my skills as a practitioner. It looked like a great business based around my talents. But around seven years ago, it became clear to me that the business had no legs. It wasn't a business; it would collapse under its own weight. In fact, it was bottom-heavy, and there were tons of payroll. But the most important realization was that the company only ran if I personally kept feeding the funnel with business.

We made a decision to slowly bring on other advisors along with more back-office capability to support them. We needed the back-office support to accommodate the increased volume, and people with different skill sets to support younger advisors. We had to help them close deals as well, because they didn't yet have experience. I hired those advisors with a low base salary and a small piece of deals. But then I brought them along to meet clients, and they learned how I approached the client relationship, which taught them the same transformational language that got a predictable result every time.

A TEAM SPORT

Today, it's a team sport at our firm. Instead of just one advisor servicing a client, we have a team of employees surrounding that advisor. Clients have relationships with four or five other people in the office. We're not pushing them off to somebody else. We're not reducing the service they receive. We're giving them another level of service.

Instead of a client feeling like they were dealing with the CEO for many years, and now they've been passed off to some inexperienced advisor, the goal in our service model is to provide a relationship so that we can do better together. Clients feel enhanced rather than shunned.

We now have six advisors who are bringing in business, in addition to me. Most of the leads still come from me, but I believe it's now possible for me to take six months off without the business being greatly affected. We would see a difference, as I'm still the top-selling advisor (which I should be after thirty-three years), but we're getting to a place where the survival of the business is not dependent on me. What's more, the long-term health of the business will not be dependent on what I do day-to-day.

The stability of our business is not based on new sales; it's centered on recurring revenue. As I said earlier, we have 3,500 clients (and growing), but we know that revenue is going to come in from those clients whether or not we sell something new. The way I budget is to make sure the recurring revenue covers all of our overhead, plus a base salary for myself. If we sold nothing new this year, nothing would change. Therefore, everything that we sell new—and we sell an awful lot of new business—goes right to the bottom line as profit. There's a lot of comfort in that.

Seven years ago, I was bringing in 100 percent of the new business. When the business revolved around my talents, it was limited by the fact that I had only 24 hours in my day. It became eminently clear to me that I did not have a business. Today, we have six other advisors who are out there in front of clients, not only keeping them happy, but also bringing in new business. Seven years ago, I did not have a business. I now have a business that pays me four ways.

CHAPTER 10

An Invitation

When we sit down with a prospective client, we ask them to think deeply about the kind of life they want *right now*. Then, we figure out a plan for them to have that life, keep it that way forever, and never run out of money.

But it all starts with a conversation about more than just finances. Because when we're talking about someone's finances, we're really talking about their life. Our goal is to gather as much information as possible—not only the numbers but who you are, how you got here, where you are trying to go, and what keeps you awake at night.

That last one is critical: *What are your deepest concerns?* Let's address those first. How can we talk about someone's finances without talking about their life? What's the money there for if not to support that person's life and their family members' lives? Most people have a black-and-white approach to finances, but how can we talk about numbers when there's something more pressing going on? We're here to have those conversations. We build bonds with our clients where there is a great deal of trust. That's what makes us unique.

HIGH-TRUST RELATIONSHIPS

A lot of people, from all different levels of wealth, think that working on their finances is a painful experience, like standing in a long line at the DMV or ripping off a bandage too quickly. It doesn't have to be. Our process is about changing that mind-set because it can, and should be, fun. We want a process where clients look forward to taking part in it—where it can be enjoyable and meaningful, where we are true partners in the plan. These become high-trust relationships.

One of the great things about my job is I'm working with friends, not acquaintances. I'm not working with people in a transactional way; I'm working to help transform our clients' lives. I don't want to control people's money. I want to help them be able to control, enjoy, and spend their wealth while living the lives they want.

If you have a financial advisor now, do you look forward to those meetings? Do you want to spend more time with that person? Do you have a plan that has great synergy?

You *can* make it something you really enjoy. It's enjoyable for us, too. It's purposeful work for everyone in the office, from the person who answers the phone to the top advisor. When you're helping people over a long period create real wealth, the conversations change. At first: "My spouse and I are trying to be secure in our retirement." Later: "Now that we're secure, let's focus on our kids being fine for the rest of their lives." And then: "Now that our kids are secure, let's make sure the grandkids will also be taken care of." Finally, after all those boxes are checked, the conversation becomes about the things that client can do to help other people and change the world.

A longtime client of ours, a doctor, has reached the point where he and his wife believe they finally have multi-generational wealth. This doctor is ready to retire earlier than planned, because they're no longer worried about having enough money. Their four children, however, all have significant student loan debt (one is a lawyer and three are doctors). Last fall, we sat down with the couple and talked about their Christmas gift to their children: "How much student loan debt do you have left?" the couple asked their children. The reply was, "I think we have around $500,000 left." And the couple said, "No, you don't. We paid it off yesterday." They were in a position to be able to do that.

Other clients realize that because of their planning they can make an impact on the lives of their grandchildren. They can spend more time with the grandkids, help with education, and take them on special trips. For longtime clients, they start thinking about the things they can do for other people and to help change the world. For example, we have a client who was born in Armenia, where there is little modern dental care. Once this client reached a certain level of financial security, he started to use his money to create mobile dental clinics in his home country.

HAVING A PLAN AND PRACTICING PROVEN STRATEGIES

Real wealth is not created by putting your money into mutual funds or any other financial product. Many people are getting the wrong advice. Financial institutions try to convince everyone that these products are where money is made. Instead of developing a long-term strategy that takes into account the client's life plan, the focus is wrongly on commodities, inflation-adjusted holding tanks, and expecting to get a high-percentage yield from the market.

Your total financial picture cannot be commoditized, yet that is still the way wealth creation is generally approached. How is that working for most people? Based on our experience with clients, very few Americans have enough passive income from assets to replace their paycheck when they stop working. The tiny percentage of people that get there indicates (1) that the generally accepted way of creating wealth has not been very successful, and (2) that planning is required.

Assets are merely inflation-adjusted holding tanks. What matters is ensuring that those assets produce highly reliable streams of income to replace your paycheck when you stop working.

* * *

What are the milestones clients are looking for in life? What are the things that we need to do? We get answers to these question and then reverse-engineer a plan to get there. Financial products are static commodities, but a plan can be revisited; it is adaptable. A plan makes sure you have liquidity available to be nimble, to move on opportunities, and to deal with the challenges that arise. That plan is fluid and open to the changes that inevitably happen in life. Progress can be monitored. With a road map in place, you know where you're headed. You know what buckets need to be filled and how that money will be used to support you and your family.

Most people simply don't have a plan at all. Many think they're going to work for thirty or forty years, put money into inflation-adjusted holding tanks, retire, and have the success they deserve—only they haven't done the things necessary to get there. It's no different than if I had never played golf in my life, and one day I pick up a golf club with the intention of winning the Masters the following year. It's not going happen. The chances are next to zero.

As we mentioned previously, 78 percent of professional athletes were either bankrupt or in severe financial distress just two years after retirement.[5] Those athletes had no plan. While the percentage of the general population in that dire position is not as high, most people are forced to make concessions in retirement. They either keep working or retire with a downgraded lifestyle.

For people who are willing to embrace our strategy, having a plan takes your chance of success from nearly zero to nearly 100 percent. Having a financial plan that considers life goals is transformational. The clients who create a plan and internalize it are ones who become successful. When it's their plan and we're partners in making sure that plan is carried out, it almost always works.

Having a financial plan that considers life goals is transformational. The clients who create a plan and internalize it are ones who become successful.

Remember, most people spend more time planning their family vacations than working on their personal finances. There's really no excuse for that. Nor is there an excuse for not practicing the parameters of wealth creation talked about in chapter 1: live within your means, save 15 percent of your gross income every year, have proper insurance, have liquidity, be your own CFO, and don't have bad debt. You must be willing to follow these commandments and practice the behaviors of people who are successful. Ultimately, it's about consistent behaviors. Even if you win the lottery or inherit a bunch of money, most people will lose that money if they don't follow these parameters.

For many clients, this starts with a mind-set shift—deciding you're going to do the work to be successful. If you can't save 15 percent of your pre-tax earnings, then let's pick a smaller number.

---

5   van Ramele, Aoki, Kerkhoffs, and Gouttebarge, op. cit.

Let's start with 3 percent if that's where we need to begin. Small steps will get you the future you want.

Our strategy empowers clients to see how their personal and financial lives can work together. You get there by living within your means, being your own CFO, and getting direction, creativity, and companionship from a financial advisor who's not just selling products.

DIRECTION, CREATIVITY, AND COMPANIONSHIP

Even with folks who do have a plan, they often do not create a real, thought-out plan that includes life goals, nor do they monitor or measure it. They don't have the capability to do it themselves, and they don't have somebody there to provide direction, creativity, and companionship. That's what we do.

We provide direction by teaching from experience. We have our own money invested, and we use the same strategies we employ with clients. The financial products that we support, we own ourselves. The strategies we employ, we use ourselves. If we don't do it, we don't teach it. You wouldn't hire personal trainer who has never exercised, right? Nor would you want a financial advisor who hasn't created independent wealth for themselves. We hammer and hammer on sound, tested theories about how to get paid four ways and create extraordinary wealth—all of which we have done ourselves.

We also bring creativity to adapt to every client's unique situation. Clients are looking for creativity from their financial advisor. Nothing too out there, of course, but certainly some resourcefulness and originality to be able to serve them to the highest level.

While the client drives the process, we offer companionship along the way. It's not about us or our lives; it's always about them and their journey. It's about making their life better. Ultimately, we're just the conduit for their journey. Our planning becomes a vessel of possibility for our clients.

Our role is providing direction, creativity, and companionship, but you're still the CFO. If you want to create extraordinary wealth, you cannot delegate your financial life to someone else. You cannot be separate from your plan. If you have a plan but don't internalize it, and if you don't hire yourself as your own CFO, and instead leave those duties up to somebody else—whether that's a wire house advisor, an accountant, or your brother-in-law—those plans have nearly as high a failure rate as having no plan at all.

If you want to create extraordinary wealth, you cannot delegate your financial life to someone else.

WHAT'S THE VALUE OF FINANCIAL STATEMENTS?

A conversation with a prospective client sometimes goes like this:

I ask, "Would you highly recommend your accountant if I was moving to your area?"

"No," the client would say (most people answer like this).

"If you wouldn't recommend them to me, why would you use them? Let's hold on that for a second. Do you get financial statements?"

"Yes," the client would say.

"Are they usually on time?"

"No, they're usually late."

"When you look at your financial statements, other than knowing what percentage you're up or down for the year, how does that help you run your business tomorrow?"

"I don't know."

So, what's the value to them? There's a better way than just having a financial advisor and what I call a "cast around" plan, which is one that says, "I want to get the kids educated, I'd like to get the house paid off, and I'd like to be able to retire at a reasonable age." Those are good goals, of course, but they're neither inspiring nor motivated by what truly drives them. They don't include things like having the time to coach their kid's baseball team or helping build a community center in their town.

HAVING A MORE PURPOSEFUL LIFE

This is your one and only life. How do we transform that life you so your vision can become your reality? So you run your life around your money and not the other way around? That's a completely different outlook than putting money in your 401(k) every pay period or giving a broker X amount to gamble in the stock market, neither of which are inspirational or aspirational. How is that transforming your life and the lives of others?

The strategies we've talked about in this book are about allowing you to have a more purposeful life. This is our approach to wealth creation at Northeast Private Client Group. We hope you're now ready to become your own CFO and start with the small steps that will build to the future you want. We invite you to reach out to us. If this book has been helpful to you, please give us a call or send an email and we'd be happy to send a free copy to someone you love.

Contributors[6]

MARK MURPHY, CLU®, CHFC®, CEO

Mark Murphy is the CEO of Northeast Private Client Group, a national financial planning and wealth management firm headquartered in Roseland, New Jersey. Murphy focuses on his clients developing a high level of emotional fitness driven by wealth creation strategies that work under all circumstances. Northeast Private Client Group provides strategic planning

---

6   Benjamin Bush, Adam Schlossberg, Michael Millman, and Christopher Viola are Registered Representatives and Financial Advisors of Park Avenue Securities LLC (PAS). OSJ: 200 Broadhollow Road Suite 405, Melville, NY 11747 (631-589-5400). Securities products and advisory services offered through PAS, member FINRA, SIPC. PAS is an indirect, wholly-owned subsidiary of Guardian. Northeast Private Client Group is not an affiliate or subsidiary of PAS or Guardian.

and financial engineering to closely held businesses, medium-sized companies, celebrities, athletes, hedge fund managers, doctors, dentists, and other high net worth individuals. Murphy speaks nationally on mergers and acquisitions, estate planning, charitable giving, and strategies to create multi-generation wealth.

ADAM SCHLOSSBERG, CFP®, PRESIDENT

Adam Schlossberg is the president of Northeast Private Client Group. He takes a personalized approach by developing, implementing, and monitoring financial and business strategies that meet the different

needs of each client. He is always willing to challenge conventional wisdom by thinking outside the box when it comes to investing and preserving wealth.

Adam holds a BS in finance and risk management from the University of Wisconsin, Madison. He holds the Series 7 and Series 66 licenses, which makes him a fiduciary to his clients, as well as life and health licenses.

Adam's continued commitment to education ensures that he is current with financial planning news, information and trends.

BENJAMIN J. BUSH, CLU®, FINANCIAL ADVISOR

Benjamin J. Bush is a financial advisor with Northeast Private Client Group. Through his work, Ben demonstrates a firm commitment to providing clients with sound, proven financial strategies that will help them maximize wealth, protect their assets, and plan for a dignified retirement.

After graduating from the University of Florida with a bachelor of science degree in psychology, Ben began his financial services career working with small business owners and individuals in South Florida. During this time, he established long-lasting relationships with a number of dental professionals. He then moved to New York and aligned with Sequoia Private Client Group in 2008. Furthering his education remains a priority for Ben, as it enables him to keep his clients informed. In addition to attaining his Chartered Life Underwriter® (CLU®) designation; the Series 66, 6, and 7; and life, health, and variable annuities sales licenses, he is currently working toward his Chartered Financial Consultant (ChFC®) designation at The American College.

Ben's strong sense of industry and community keep him actively involved as a member of various professional and civic organizations, including Americans for Financial Security (AFS), the National Association of the Self-Employed (NASE), the Association of Insurance and Financial Advisors, the Estate Planning Council of New York City, the Accountants' Club of America, the Million Dollar Roundtable, and Court of the Table. Ben remains philanthropically involved by supporting various organizations, such as the Children's Heart Foundation, the American Heart Association, the National MS Society, Children's International, and New York-Presbyterian Hospital. In his free time, Ben enjoys playing golf, tennis, and spending time with his wife, Stephanie, and two children, Layla and Ethan.

MICHAEL MILLMAN, FINANCIAL ADVISOR

Michael Millman graduated from the University of Miami School of Business Administration with a BBA focusing on finance, entrepreneurship, and business law disciplines. He will be pursuing an MBA and his CFP® designation. He has been helping clients exponentially grow their businesses and wealth since. His background provides him with a philosophical, perceptive, and nuanced approach to wealth creation.

He is a fourth-generation financial advisor who not only helps clients perfect their "financial swing," but who also deeply develops relationships to last a lifetime.

Michael is on the forefront of the latest strategies, techniques, and technologies to ensure that clients' plans are always taking advantage of an ever-evolving environment. He has expert knowledge in advanced case design, insurance, investments, estate planning, and business growth strategies. He is Series 7 and Series 66 licensed, and also holds life, health, and variable annuity sales licenses in all states.

Michael is an innovative thinker that loves to look outside of the box and between the numbers so his clients can achieve what they thought to be impossible.

In his free time, Michael is an avid scuba diver and enjoys hiking, running, and competing in various fitness challenges. He is also a certified personal trainer who loves to workout and design fitness and nutrition plans. To relax, he loves to read, meditate, and discover new music.

CHRISTOPHER G. VIOLA, FINANCIAL ADVISOR

Christopher Viola is a financial advisor at Northeast Private Client Group in Roseland, New Jersey, and has been working in the financial industry for six years, originally at JP Morgan Chase. He was inspired to pursue a career in financial services due to his fascination with the financial markets, coupled with his innate desire to help people. Chris specializes in retirement planning, investments, and insurance, with a unique ability to deliver individual attention and superior customer service.

Chris is from Westchester, New York, but currently resides with his family in Chatham, New Jersey. In his free time, he enjoys reading, basketball, football, and weight lifting.

SEPEHR ARAGHI, FINANCIAL ADVISOR

Born and raised in the San Francisco Bay Area, Sepehr joined Northeast Private Client Group as an associate in August 2018 and specializes in retirement planning and insurance. Growing up, Sepehr's parents instilled in him a strong sense of ethics and caring for others.

Sepehr believes that by knowing and understanding a client on a holistic level, rather than simply by their professional life, he can offer strategies that not only provide clients financial freedom personally, but that also help realize and achieve their professional dreams.

Being surrounded by like-minded business professionals, Sepehr has developed a unique mind-set that fits perfectly within Sequoia, and is part of the team that creates strategies and plans used to help grow businesses of all types.

He holds a bachelor of science degree in economics with a minor in entrepreneurship from Santa Clara University.

Disclosure